YOU ARE MY FRIEND

*As I love nature, as I love
singing birds, and morning,
and evening, and summer, I
love thee, my friend.*
Henry David Thoreau

FOR MY FRIEND,

_____
To

*A friend may well be reckoned the
masterpiece of nature.*
Proverbs

_____
From

YOU ARE MY FRIEND

A CELEBRATION OF FRIENDSHIP

Compiled By
THE EDITORS OF HALO BOOKS

With
A FRIENDSHIP SAMPLER
By
HAL LARSON

HALO BOOKS
SAN FRANCISCO, CALIFORNIA

Designed By Susan Larson

Library of Congress Cataloging-in-Publication Data

You are my friend: a celebration of friendship

Compiled by the editors of Halo Books;
with a friendship sampler by Hal Larson.

Includes index.
I. Friendship—Literary collections. 1. Larson, Hal, 1924-.
II. Halo Books (Firm)
PN6071.F7Y68 1991   808.8'0353   90-5028
ISBN 0-9622874-8-2

Published by Halo Books
P.O. Box 2529, San Francisco, CA 94126
Typography by BookPrep
Manufactured in the United States of America
Library of Congress Catalog Card Number 90-5028
International Standard Book Number 0-9622874-8-2

CONTENTS

A Friendship Sampler

By Hal Larson

"What a thing friendship is," Browning wrote, "world without end."

Emerson agreed: "A friend may well be reckoned the masterpiece of nature." And Grimoald posed the rhetorical "Of all the heavenly gifts that mortal men commend, what trusty treasure can countervail a friend?"

Friendship enobles us, fulfills us, even cures our ills. "A faithful friend," proclaimes Ecclesiaticus, "is the medicine of life." And that medicine is ours for the giving.

You Are My Friend

Life's richest treasure, friendship. It warms our soul as the sun does our body. Without it, the world would be a forbidding place.

We know these things. Yet precious as friendship is, few of us are comfortable expressing it. We just don't know how to give words to this sweet and tender thing.

Happily for us, others have walked here before. From Cicero—"It's like taking the sun out of the world to bereave human life of friendship."—to James Taylor—"Ain't it good to know you've got a friend?"— thinkers and poets have illuminated this elusive magic that Young called "the wine of life."

How do you say "You are my friend?" Assembled in these pages is a chorus of voices resonating to that timeless wonderment. They sing of friendship's strength, its integrity and purity. They fill our hearts with the elegant harmony of friendship.

Shakespeare, as always, said it most efficiently: "He was my friend, faithful and just to me." And as usual, Dickens put it most unpredictably: "May we never want a friend in need, nor a bottle to give him."

But it is Thoreau who stirs our soul: "As I love nature, as I love singing birds, and morning and evening, and summer, and winter, I love thee, my friend."

Friendship Sampler

I love thee, my friend!" "True love and friendship are the same." wrote James Thompson. And much earlier, Epictetus advised "Let no man think he is loved by any man when he loves no man."

"And we find at the end of a perfect day," mused Carrie Jacobs Bond, "the soul of a friend we've made." Aristotle observed "Friendship is one mind in two bodies."

Though friendship is itself indivisible, this collection of friendship lyrics is divided into a dozen sections.

In the first section, *The Essentials of Friendship*, we see Southerne advising " 'T is something to be willing to commend; but my best praise is that I am your friend." And a stern George Washington announces to a citizen "I will deal with you with all the frankness which is due to friendship."

Anais Nin confesses "What I cannot love, I overlook. Is that," she asks "real friendship?" Corrine Roosevelt Robinson suggests "Though love be deeper, friendship is more wide."

And Emily Brontë poses this thought:
Love is like the wild rose-briar;
    Friendship like the holly tree.
The holly is dark when the rose-briar blooms,
    But which will bloom most constantly?

You Are My Friend

The Path To Friendship, the second section, has Theodore Munger advising us to "Choose a friend as thou dost a wife, till death separates you." Henry Wallace suggests "Seek no friend to make him useful, for that is the negation of friendship; but seek him that you may be useful, for this is of friendship's essence."

"Treat your friends as you do your pictures," wrote Jennie Churchill, "and place them in their best light." Simone Weil points out "To want friendship is a great fault. Friendship ought to be a gratuitous joy."

And George Eliot notes "Friendships begin with liking or gratitude—roots that can be pulled up."

Cicero tells us in the same section that "Friendship springs from nature rather than need." And J.R. Miller says "wanting to have a friend is altogether different from wanting to be a friend."

The third section, *The Barriers To Friendship*, has Moliere reporting "An indisicriminate heart's regard I scorn—myself must needs be prized; in brief the friend of all mankind's no friend for me." Coco Chanel says "My friends, there are no friends."

Mark Twain volunteers "The holy passion of friendship is of so sweet and steady and loyal and enduring a nature, that it will last through a whole lifetime, if not asked to lend money."

[x]

Friendship Sampler

James Russell Lowell adds "I don't meddle with what my friends believe or reject any more than I ask whether they are rich or poor; I love them." And from William Hazlitt: "There are no rules to friendship. It must be left to itself; we cannot force it any more than love."

Section Four, *Being a Friend,* includes this from George Bancroft: "The friendship between you and me I will not compare to a chain; for that the rains might rust, or the falling tree break."

George Eliot slides in with "Animals are such agreeable friends—they ask no questions, they pass no criticisms." Mary Catherwood observes "Two may talk under the same roof for many years, yet never really meet; and two others at first speech are old friends."

From Carole King:
> Winter, spring, summer or fall
> all you have to do is call
> And I'll be there,
> You've got a friend.

"What's the good of money if it ain't to help a friend out with?" asks Henry Wallace Phillips. "I believe in friends, I do. Here we go hopping around this world for a small time, and then that's done. S'pose you ain't got any real friends for the trip? Rotten, I say."

You Are My Friend

Victor Hugo, in *Being Befriended,* Section Five, writes "The greatest happiness in life is the conviction that we are loved, loved for ourselves, or rather loved in spite of ourselves." Dickens says "Be a friend; the rest will follow."

"We talk of taxes," wrote Edna St. Vincent Millay, "and I call you friend." Lady Montagu observed "I'm very lonely now—for the poor make no new friends."

Sarah Ellis: "To act the part of a true friend requires more conscientious feeling than to fill with credit and complacency any other station or capacity in life."

Emerson puts it simply: "O be my friend, and teach me to be thine."

In the sixth section *The Advice Of Friends,* Edward George Bulwer-Lytton notes "There is no man so friendless but what he can find a friend sincere enough to tell him disagreeable truths."

Harriet Beecher Stowe: "I am speaking now of the highest duty we owe our friends, the nobleness, goodness, pure and incorrupt . . . If we *let* our friends become cold and selfish and exacting without a remonstrance, we are no true lover, no true friend."

And Richard Brinsley offers "If it is abuse—why one is always sure to hear of it from one damned good-natured friend or other."

Friendship Sampler

Tennyson, in Section Seven, *Friends and Enemies,* tells us "He makes no friend who never made a foe", a thought echoed by William Hazlitt: "He will never have true friends who is afraid of making enemies."

"The richer your friends," observes Elisabeth Marbury, "the more they will cost you." And Gertrude Stein says "Before the flowers of friendship faded friendship faded."

"God preserve me from my friends" says an Italian proverb; "from my enemies I will preserve myself." And William Cowper wrote "Thy friendship has made my heart to ache; do be my enemy for friendship's sake."

Men and Women Friends, Section Eight, includes this from Cornelius Whurr: "What lasting joys the man attend who has a polished female friend." Samuel Taylor Coleridge suggests "A woman's friendship borders more closely on love than a man's."

"My true friends," reflects Colette, "have always given me that supreme proof of devotion, a spontaneous aversion for the man I loved."

Lord Byron, who knew a thing or two about the subject, weighs in with sobering wisdom: "I have always laid it down as a maxim, and found it justified by experience, that a man and a woman make better friendships than can exist between two of the same sex; but with this condition, that they never have made, or are to make, love with each other."

More on this engaging kind of friendship from Francois de Rochefoulcauld: "The reason why so many women are touched by friendship is that they find it dull when they have experienced love."

Section Nine, *Friends and Relations,* a shade less exotic to most of us, includes the Proverb "A good friend is better than a near relation." Cicero puts it shortly: "Friendship excells relationship."

An adaptation of George Ade: "A child may be an affliction, or a parent a misfortune; but a friend is a man's own fault."

An Italian proverb holds: "Better one true friend than a host of kinfolk." And the Book of Proverbs echos: "Better be a neighbor that is near than a brother far off."

In the tenth section, *Old Friends,* Caroline Norton reminisces "We have been friends together in sunshine and in shade." and Dorothy Parker reflects "Constant use had not worn ragged the fabric of their friendship."

And the redoubtable Sarah Orne Jewett: "Yes'm, old friends is always best, 'less you can catch a new one that's fit to make an old one out of."

Friendship Sampler

Francis Bacon remembers "Alonso of Aragon was wont to say in commendation of age, that age appears to be best in four things, old wood to burn, old wine to drink, old friends to trust, and old authors to read." A knowing proverb holds "The best mirror is an old friend."

"An old friend may be often found and lost," mused Samuel Johnson, "but an old friend can never be found, and nature has provided that he cannot be easily lost."

The Eleventh Section, *Friendship Remembered*, recalls Seneca's wisdom, "The comfort of having a friend may be taken away, but not that of having had one." Also the melancholy comment of Thomas Jefferson, "Near friends, falling out, never reunite cordially."

Emerson wrote "Let the soul be assured that somewhere in the universe it shall rejoin its friend, and it will be content and cheerful alone for a thousand years." Dinah Clark asks "Friend, what years could us divide?"

Christina Rossetti:
My friends had failed one by one,
    Middle-aged, young, and old,
Till the ghosts were warmer to me
    Than my friends that had grown cold.

You Are My Friend

And there is the captivating conundrum from John Rioux: "We call that person who has lost his father an orphan; and a widower, that man who has lost his wife. And that man who has known that immense unhappiness of losing his friend, by what name do we call him? Here every human language holds its peace in omnipotence."

The final section, *In Praise Of Friends* has James Howell disclaiming "Friendship is the great chain of human society." And Count von Platen holds "Love is deemed the tenderest of our affections, as even the blind and deaf know; but I know, what few believe, that true friendship is more tender still."

From Elizabeth Shane: "But every road is rough to him that has no friend to share it." And Opal Whiteley notes: "It is such a comfort to have a friend near, when lonesome feels do come."

Charles Diddin brags "In every mess I finds a friend, In every port a wife." And Young concludes "Angels from friendship gather half their joys."

Drink joyfully from the heady wine stored here. You will find something for every occasion and every mood.

Now no longer need you struggle for the words to express your friendship. Select from the rich menu in these pages. Or simply give a copy to your friend.

[xvi]

YOU ARE
MY FRIEND

1
THE ESSENTIALS OF FRIENDSHIP

A man that hath friends must show himself friendly: and there is a friend that sticketh closer than a brother.

— *Proverbs of Solomon*

———— • ♦ • ————

Friendship is one mind in two bodies.

— *Aristotle*

———— • ♦ • ————

Only a wise man knows how to love; only a wise man is a friend.

— *Seneca*

———— • ♦ • ————

Let us, then, be what we are and speak what we think, and in all
Keep ourselves loyal to truth, and the sacred professions of friendship.

— *Henry Wadsworth Longfellow*

You Are My Friend

A very simple intellectual mechanism answers the necessities of friendship, and even of the most intimate relations of life. If a watch tells us the hour and minute, we can be content to carry it about with us for a lifetime, though it has no second hand and is not a repeater, nor a musical watch, though it is not enameled nor jeweled,—in short though it has little beyond the wheels required for a trustworthy instrument, added to a good face and a pair of useful hands.

— Oliver Wendell Holmes

———— • ◆ • ————

I will deal with you with all the frankness which is due to friendship.

— George Washington

———— • ◆ • ————

A benevolent man should allow a few faults in himself, to keep his friends in countenance.

— Benjamin Franklin

———— • ◆ •. ————

How were friendship possible? In mutual devotedness to the Good and True: otherwise impossible except as armed neutrality or hollow commercial league.

— Thomas Carlyle

The Essentials of Friendship

Friendship above all ties does bind the heart;
And faith in friendship is the noblest part.
— *Earl of Orrey*

———— • ♦ • ————

We talk of choosing friends, but friends are self-elected.
— *Ralph Waldo Emerson*

———— • ♦ • ————

What makes a friend? The heart that glows
With changeless love in Arctic snows,
Nor fails to cheer 'mid desert sand.
This plainer speaks than clasp of hand:
Hands may be firmly clasped by foes.
— *Volney Streamer*

———— • ♦ • ————

I love a friendship free and frank.
— *John Byrom*

———— • ♦ • ————

True friendship cannot be among many.
— *Norris*

———— • ♦ • ————

Beautiful friendship, tried by sun and wind,
Durable from the daily dust of life.
— *Stephen Phillips*

[3]

You Are My Friend

The essence of friendship is entireness, a total magnanimity and trust. It must not surmise or provide for infirmity. It treats its object as a god, that it may deify both.

— *Ralph Waldo Emerson*

——— • ◆ • ———

Think it not friendship which forever seeks itself; but that which gives itself for others.

— *Perry Marshall*

——— • ◆ • ———

It is well that there is no one without a fault, for he would not have a friend in the world.

— *William Hazlitt*

——— • ◆ • ———

'T is thus in friendship; who depend
On many rarely find a friend.

— *John Gay*

——— • ◆ • ———

A true friend unbosoms freely, advises justly, assists readily, adventures boldly, takes all patiently, defends courageously, and continues a friend unchangeably.

— *William Penn*

The Essentials of Friendship

The laws of friendship are great, austere, and eternal, of one web with the laws of nature and of morals.

— *Ralph Waldo Emerson*

——— • ◆ • ———

Friendship should be surrounded with ceremonies and respect, and not crushed into corners. Friendship requires more time than poor busy man can usually command.

— *Ralph Waldo Emerson*

——— • ◆ • ———

True happiness
Consists not in the multitude of friends,
But in the worth and choice.

— *Ben Jonson*

——— • ◆ • ———

A true test of friendship, to sit or walk with a friend for an hour in perfect silence without wearying of one another's company.

— *Dinah Muloch*

——— • ◆ • ———

It is not enough to love those who are near and dear to us. We must show them that we do so.

— *Lord Avebury*

[5]

You Are My Friend

In friendship there is nothing pretended, nothing feigned, whatever there is in it is both genuine and spontaneous.

— *Cicero*

——— • ◆ • ———

Everything that is mine, even to my life, I may give to one I love, but the secret of my friend is not mine to give.

— *Sir Philip Sidney*

——— • ◆ • ———

True friendship in two breasts requires
The same aversions, and desires.
— *Jonathan Swift*

——— • ◆ • ———

I wish that friendship should have feet, as well as eyes and eloquence. It must plant itself on the ground, before it walks over the moon. I wish it to be a little of a citizen, before it is quite a cherub.

— *Ralph Waldo Emerson*

——— • ◆ • ———

A crowd is not company, and faces are but a gallery of pictures, and talk but a tinkling cymbal, where there is no love.

— *Francis Bacon*

The Essentials of Friendship

A generous friendship no cold medium knows,
Burns with one love, with one resentment glows.
— *Alexander Pope*

———— • ◆ • ————

We must not expect our friends to be above humanity.

— *Ouida*

———— • ◆ • ————

I do not treat friendships daintily, but with roughest courage. When they are real, they are not glass threads or frost work, but the solidest thing we know.

— *Ralph Waldo Emerson*

———— • ◆ • ————

All men have their frailties, and whoever looks for a friend without imperfections will never find what he seeks. We love ourselves notwithstanding our faults, and we ought to love our friends in like manner.

— *Cyrus*

———— • ◆ • ————

Friendship's true laws are by this rule exprest,
Welcome the coming, speed the parting guest.
— *Alexander Pope*

[7]

You Are My Friend

Nay, my lords, ceremony was but devised at first
To set a gloss on faint deeds, hollow welcomes,
Recanting goodness, sorry ere 't is shown;
But where there is true friendship, there needs none.
                                    — *William Shakespeare*

——— • ♦ • ———

The man that knows
Receiving good to render good again,
Would be a friend worth more than land or goods.
                                    — *Sophocles*

——— • ♦ • ———

Let No man think he is loved by any man when he
loves no man.
                                    — *Epictetus*

——— • ♦ • ———

In the first place, you will never have more than
two or three friends in the whole course of your life.
Your entire confidence is their right; to give it to
many is to betray those who are indeed your friends.
                                    — *Honoré de Balzac*

——— • ♦ • ———

The only reward of virtue, is virtue: The only way
to have a friend, is to be one.
                                    — *Ralph Waldo Emerson*

[8]

The Essentials of Friendship

People who always receive you with great cordiality rarely care for you. Your true friends make you a partaker of their humors.

— Manley Pike

———— • ♦ • ————

Wealth, title, office are no recommendations to my friendship. On the contrary, great good qualities are requisite to make amends for their having wealth, title, and office.

— Thomas Jefferson

———— • ♦ • ————

Friendship cannot become permanent unless it becomes spiritual. There must be fellowship in the deepest things of the soul, community in the highest thoughts, sympathy with the best endeavors.

— Hugh Black

———— • ♦ • ————

A friend should bear his friend's infirmities.

— William Shakespeare

———— • ♦ • ————

The happiness of love is in action; its test is what one is willing to do for others.

— Lew Wallace

[9]

You Are My Friend

It is only the great-hearted who can be true friends; the mean and the cowardly can never know what true friendship is.

— *Charles Kingsley*

——— • ◆ • ———

Friendship is affluent and generous, and not disposed to keep strict watch lest it may give more than it receives.

— *Cicero*

——— • ◆ • ———

Ah, friend! to dazzle let the vain design;
To raise the thought and touch the heart be thine.
— *Alexander Pope*

——— • ◆ • ———

What I cannot love, I overlook. Is that real friendship.

— *Anais Nin*

——— • ◆ • ———

If one's intimate in love or friendship cannot or does not share all one's intellectual tastes or pursuits, that is a small matter. Intellectual companions can be found easily in men and books. After all, if we think of it, most of the world's great loves and friendships have been between people that could not read or spell.

— *Oliver Wendell Holmes*

[10]

The Essentials of Friendship

Once a man came and knocked at the door of his friend.
His friend said, "Who art thou, O faithful one?"
He said "'T is I." He answered, "There is no admittance.
There is no room for the raw at my well-cooked feast.
Naught but fire and separation and absence
Can cook the raw one and free him from the hypocrisy!
Since thy self has not yet left thee,
Thou must be burned in fiery flames."

The poor man went away, and for one whole year
Journeyed burning with grief for his friend's absence.
His heart burned till it was cooked; then he went again
And drew near to the house of his friend.
He knocked at the door in fear and trepidation
Lest some careless word should fall from his lips.
His friend shouted, "Who is at the door?"
He answered, "'T is thou who art at the door, O beloved!"
The friend said, "Since 't is I, let me come in,
There is not room for two I's in one house."
      — *From the Masnavi of Jelalud-din Rumi*

———— • ◆ • ————

A mutual understanding is ever the firmest chain.
      — *Ralph Waldo Emerson*

———— • ◆ • ————

The question was once put to Aristotle, how we ought to behave to our friends; and the answer he gave was, "As we should wish our friends to behave to us."

      — *Plutarch*

[11]

You Are My Friend

True love and friendship are the same.
— *James Thomson*

———— • ◆ • ————

Friendship, like love, is but a name,
Unless to one you stint the flame.
The child whom many fathers share
Hath seldom known a father's care.
'T is thus in friendship—who depend
On many rarely find a friend.
— *John Gay*

———— • ◆ • ————

A slender acquaintance with the world must convince every man, that actions, not words, are the true criterion of the attachment of friends; and that the most liberal profession of good-will is very far from being the surest mark of it.
— *George Washington*

———— • ◆ • ————

Though love be deeper, friendship is more wide.
— *Corrine Roosevelt Robinson*

[12]

2
THE PATH TO FRIENDSHIP

'T is thus that on the choice of friends
Our good or evil name depends.
— *John Gay*

———— • ♦ • ————

In many cases of friendship, or what passes for it, the old axiom is reversed, and like clings to unlike more than to like.

— *Charles Dickens*

———— • ♦ • ————

Friendship is no plant of hasty growth;
Though planted in esteem's deep fixed soil,
The gradual culture of kind intercourse
Must bring it to perfection.
— *Joanna Baillie*

———— • ♦ • ————

From wine what sudden friendship springs!
— *John Gay*

[13]

You Are My Friend

Make me to love my feller-man
   Yea, though his bitterness
Doth bite as only adders can
   Let me the fault confess,
And go to him and clasp his hand,
   And love him none the less.
So keep me, Lord, forever free
   From vane concete with him,
And he whose pius eyes can see
   My faults, however dim,
Oh! let him pray the least fer me,
   And me the most fer him.
            — *James Whitcomb Riley*

———— • ◆ • ————

Choose a friend as thou dost a wife, till death separates you.

            — *Theodore Munger*

———— • ◆ • ————

Seek no friend to make him useful, for that is the negation of friendship; but seek him that you may be useful, for this is of friendship's essence.

            — *Henry Wallace*

———— • ◆ • ————

Yet how often we know merely the sight of those we call our friends, or the sound of their voices, but nothing whatever of their mind or soul.

            — *Lord Avebury*

[14]

The Path to Friendship

Be slow in choosing a friend, slower in changing.
— *Benjamin Franklin*

———— • ◆ • ————

Friendship is certainly the finest balm for pangs of disappointed love.

— *Jane Austen*

———— • ◆ • ————

Turn him and see his threads, look if he be
Friend to himself, that would be friend to thee,
For that is first required, a man to be his own;
But he that's too much that, is friend to none.
— *Ben Jonson*

———— • ◆ • ————

A good man is the best friend, and therefore soonest to be chosen, longest to be retained; and indeed never to be parted with, unless he cease to be that for which he was chosen.

— *Jeremy Taylor*

———— • ◆ • ————

Some seem to make a man a friend, or try to do so, because he lives near, because he is in the same business, travels on the same line of railway, or for some other trivial reason. There cannot be a greater mistake.

— *Lord Avebury*

[15]

You Are My Friend

These friends thou hast, and their adoption tried,
Grapple them to thy soul with hoops of steel.
— *William Shakespeare*

———— • ◆ • ————

Friendships are discovered rather than made.
— *Harriet Beecher Stowe*

———— • ◆ • ————

When we live through love we begin friendship.
— *Heinrich Heine*

———— • ◆ • ————

Friendship made in a moment is of no moment.
— *Proverb*

———— • ◆ • ————

Choose your companions wisely, and your friends
will come about naturally.
— *Theodore Munger*

———— • ◆ • ————

Our chief want in life is, somebody who shall
make us do what we can. This is the service of a
friend.

— *Ralph Waldo Emerson*

[16]

The Path to Friendship

Friendship springs from nature rather than from need.

— Cicero

———— • ◆ • ————

A decent boldness ever meets with friends.
— Alexander Pope

———— • ◆ • ————

Every man should have a fair sized cemetery in which to bury the faults of his friends.

— Henry Ward Beecher

———— • ◆ • ————

As I love nature, as I love singing birds, and gleaming stubble, and flowing rivers, and morning, and evening, and summer, and winter, I love thee, my friend.

— Henry David Thoreau

———— • ◆ • ————

Blessed are they who have the gift of making friends, for it is one of God's best gifts. It involves many things, but, above all, the power of going out of one's self, and appreciating whatever is noble and loving in another.

— Thomas Hughes

[17]

You Are My Friend

Think of this doctrine—that reasoning beings were created for one another's sake; that to be patient is a branch of justice, and that men sin without intending it.

— *Marcus Aurelius*

———— • ♦ • ————

If we would build on a sure foundation in friendship, we must love our friends for their sakes rather than for our own.

— *Charlotte Brontë*

———— • ♦ • ————

Open to me thy heart of heart's deep core,
    Or never say that I am dear to thee;
Call me not Friend, if thou keep close the door
    That leads into thine inmost sympathy.

— *James Russell Lowell*

———— • ♦ • ————

Do not let your self-love make you suppose that people become your friends at first sight, or even upon short acquaintance.

— *Lord Chesterfield*

———— • ♦ • ————

Cultivate friendliness, for it is the seed of friendship
— *Amy C. Price*

[18]

The Path to Friendship

Suspicion is well in its place, but one cultivates it at the expense of friendliness. And it is better to have friends than suspicions.

— *Bruce Henderson*

———— • ◆ • ————

The prime requisite in a good friend is the habit of good impulses

— *H.C. Chatfield-Taylor*

———— • ◆ • ————

Have friends of your own trade that shop-talk may make you skillful; have friends in other trades lest shop-talk leave you unskillful.

— *John J. Warner*

———— • ◆ • ————

An affectionate disposition is the soil in which friendship roots itself most quickly and most deeply.

— *Frances F. Graves*

———— • ◆ • ————

If you have a vice and would rid yourself of it, take for your friends those who have it not.

— *George C. Johnston*

You Are My Friend

What are the best days in memory? Those in which we met a companion who was truly such.
— *Ralph Waldo Emerson*

———— • ♦ • ————

When thine heart goeth out to a man seek not to call it back, for it is better in the keeping of a friend than in thine own.
— *Christopher Bannister*

———— • ♦ • ————

There is no virtue in a man that does not make him a better friend; no vice that does not make him worse.
— *Oliver M. Gale*

———— • ♦ • ————

It is a wise man who shares his reading with those he loves, since the more friends have in common the friendlier they are certain to be.
— *Christopher Banister*

———— • ♦ • ————

Remembering that happiness is a prime requisite to usefulness, you will be assured that friends conduce both to happiness and usefulness.
— *Brewster Matthews*

The Path to Friendship

Nature teaches beasts to know their friends.
— *William Shakespeare*

———— • ◆ • ————

There are men born for friendship, men to whom the cultivation of it is nature, is necessity.
— *Walter Savage Landor*

———— • ◆ • ————

Nothing strengthens friendship more than for one friend to feel himself the superior of the other.
— *Honoré de Balzac*

———— • ◆ • ————

Take the lid from off your heart and let me see within;
Curious, I, and impudent, a rugged man of sin.
And yet I hold you truer than president or priest;
I put my bowl against your lip and seat you at my feast;
I probe your wound and chafe your limbs and get my god to see
That you are strengthened as we fare the forest and the lea.
Strike hands with me, the glasses brim, the sun is on the heather,
And love is good and life is long and two are best together.
— *Edward Wightman*

———— • ◆ • ————

Wanting to have a friend is altogether different from wanting to be a friend.
— *J.R. Miller*

You Are My Friend

It is delicious to behold the face of a friendly and sweet person.

— Euripides

——— • ◆ • ———

Friendship is a plant which cannot be forced. True friendship is no gourd, springing in a night and withering in a day.

— Charlotte Brontë

——— • ◆ • ———

Every modern man must be many-sided; for every side he needs a friend.

— George Roberts

——— • ◆ • ———

Study yourself until you know where you are strong and where weak; study your acquaintance until you find a man weak where you are strong and strong where you are weak, that the benefits may be reciprocal; and make that man your friend.

— Robert L. Lorimer

——— • ◆ • ———

In all things be courteous to thy friend, as to thyself; for is he not thy better self?

— Christopher Bannister

The Path to Friendship

Take to your heart no friend whose affection requires proof; proof implies doubt, and where doubt is, love is not.

— Jacob de Groot

——— • ◆ • ———

Rejoice in all the honors which come to those you know. That you know them makes you, in a sense, a partner in their fame; that you rejoice with them brings you their friendship.

— Henry Worthington

——— • ◆ • ———

To distrust a friend is a double folly; for why did you take for friend one that could be distrusted? and why do you keep him? Trust IS friendship.

— Bryant A. Wooster

——— • ◆ • ———

Treat your friends as you do your pictures and place them in their best light.

— Jennie Churchill

——— • ◆ • ———

To want friendship is a great fault. Friendship ought to be a gratuitous joy.

— Simone Weil

3
THE BARRIERS TO FRIENDSHIP

He who bereaves friendship of mutual respect takes from it its greatest ornament.

— Cicero

———— • ♦ • ————

You should know the customs of a friend, but not take a dislike to them.

— Proverb

———— • ♦ • ————

That man may last, but never lives,
Who much receives but nothing gives;
Whom none can love, whom none can thank,
Creation's blot, creation's blank.
— Thomas Gibbons

———— • ♦ • ————

The better the lover, the poorer the friend.
— John Holden

[25]

You Are My Friend

An indiscriminating heart's regard
I scorn—myself must needs be prized; in brief,
The friend of all mankind's no friend for me.
> — *Molière*

———— • ◆ • ————

Keep well thy tongue and keep thy friends.
> — *Chaucer*

———— • ◆ • ————

The constitutional differences which always exist, and are obstacles to a perfect friendship, are forever a forbidden theme to the lips of friends.
> — *Henry David Thoreau*

———— • ◆ • ————

Mutual respect implies discretion and reserve even in love itself; it means preserving as much liberty as possible to those whose life we share. We must distrust our instinct of intervention, for the desire to make our own will prevail is often disguised under the mask of solicitude.
> — *From Amiel's Journal*

———— • ◆ • ————

Every friendship which a man may have becomes precarious as soon as he engages in politics.
> — *Lord Avebury*

The Barriers to Friendship

There are cases where men are so self-absorbed, so self-centered, that they take the friendship of others, their kindly thoughts and friendly deeds, without return.

— Edward Everett Hale

——— • ◆ • ———

There is nothing more fatal to friendship than the greed of gain.

— Cicero

——— • ◆ • ———

Few men have the strength to honor a friend's success without envy. I know well that mirror of friendship, shadow of a shade.

— Aeschylus

——— • ◆ • ———

The holy passion of friendship is of so sweet and steady and loyal and enduring a nature, that it will last through a whole lifetime, if not asked to lend money.

— Mark Twain

——— • ◆ • ———

Who seeks a faultless friend rests friendless.

— Turkish Proverb

You Are My Friend

Few things are more fatal to friendship than the stiffness which cannot take a step towards acknowledgment.

— *Rendel Harris*

——— • ◆ • ———

I never consider a difference of opinion in politics, in religion, in philosophy, as cause for withdrawing from a friend.

— *Thomas Jefferson*

——— • ◆ • ———

I don't meddle with what my friends believe or reject any more than I ask whether they are rich or poor; I love them.

— *James Russell Lowell*

——— • ◆ • ———

If I had the inclination and ability to do the cruelest thing upon earth to the man I hated, I would lay him under the necessity of borrowing money from a friend.

— *Edward Moore*

——— • ◆ • ———

Flattery
Is monstrous in a true friend.
— *John Ford*

The Barriers to Friendship

Friendship is usually treated by the majority of mankind as a tough and everlasting thing which will survive all manner of bad treatment. But this is an exeedingly great and foolish error; it may die in an hour of a single unwise word.

— *Ouida*

———— • ♦ • ————

As adulterine metals retain the luster and color of gold, but not the value; so flattery in imitation of friendship, takes the face and outside of it.

—*Jeremy Taylor*

———— • ♦ • ————

It is equally impossible to forget our friends, and to make them answer to our ideal. When they say farewell, then indeed we begin to keep them company. How often we find ourselves turning our back on our actual friends, that we may keep company with their ideal cousins.

— *Henry David Thoreau*

———— • ♦ • ————

Make no friendship with an angry man; and with a furious man thou shalt not go; lest thou learn his ways, and get a snare to thy soul.

— *Proverbs*

You Are My Friend

Friendship does better please our friends than flattery.
— *Jeremy Taylor*

———— • ◆ • ————

Criticism often takes from the tree caterpillars and blossoms together.
— *Author Unknown*

———— • ◆ • ————

May none whom I love to so great riches rise
As to slight their acquaintance and their old friends despise;
So low or so high may none of them be
As to move either pity or envy in me.
— *Walter Pope*

———— • ◆ • ————

Discord harder is to end than to begin.
— *Edmund Spenser*

———— • ◆ • ————

That is a miserable arithmetic which could estimate friendship as nothing, or at less than nothing.
— *Thomas Jefferson*

———— • ◆ • ————

Shall I give up the friend I have valued and tried;
If he kneel not before the same altar with me?
— *Thomas Moore*

The Barriers to Friendship

Don't flatter yourself that friendship authorizes you to say disagreeable things to your intimates.
— *Oliver Wendell Holmes*

———— • ◆ • ————

The cultivation of the friendship of a powerful man is sweet to the inexperienced; an experienced man dreads it.

— *Horace*

———— • ◆ • ————

Reserve or censure come not near
Our sacred friendship, lest there be
No solace left for thee and me.
— *Percy Bysshe Shelley*

———— • ◆ • ————

In certain circumstances in life we can bear no more from a friend than to feel him beside us. Spoken consolation irritates the wound and reveals its depth.
— *Honoré de Balzac*

———— • ◆ • ————

There are no rules for friendship. It must be left to itself; we cannot force it any more than love.
— *William Hazlitt*

You Are My Friend

The language of friendship is not words, but meanings. it is an intelligence above language.
— *Henry David Thoreau*

————— • ♦ • —————

Friendship does not confer any privilege to make ourselves disagreeable.
— *Lord Avebury*

————— • ♦ • —————

Suspicion is the bane of friendship.
— *Petrarch*

————— • ♦ • —————

Let not the grass grow on the path of friendship.
— *Proverb*

4
BEING A FRIEND

Love all, trust few,
Do wrong to none: be able for thine enemy
Rather in power than in use; and keep thy friend
Under thy own life's key.
— *William Shakespeare*

———— • ◆ • ————

There is an idea abroad among moral people that they should make their neighbors good. One person I have to make good: myself. But my duty to my neighbor is much more nearly expressed by saying that I have to make him happy—if I may.
— *Robert Louis Stevenson*

———— • ◆ • ————

My friend is not perfect—no more am I—and so we suit each other admirably.
— *Alexander Pope*

———— • ◆ • ————

Short accounts make long friends.
— *Honoré de Balzac*

You Are My Friend

"I would go up to the gates of hell with a friend,
   Through thick and thin."
The other said, as he bit off a concha end,
   "I would go in."
                                        — *John Ernest McCann*

——— • ♦ • ———

Neither is life long enough for friendship.
                              — *Ralph Waldo Emerson*

——— • ♦ • ———

My friend is that one whom I may associate with my choicest thoughts.
                              — *Henry David Thoreau*

——— • ♦ • ———

Happy is the house that shelters a friend! It might well be built, like a festal bower or arch, to entertain him for a single day.
                              — *Ralph Waldo Emerson*

——— • ♦ • ———

As ships meet at sea,—a moment together, when words of greeting must be spoken, and then away upon the deep,—so men meet in this world; and I think we should cross no man's path without hailing him, and if he needs, giving him supplies.
                              — *Henry Ward Beecher*

Being A Friend

The social, friendly, honest man,
   Wate'er he be,
'T is he fulfills great Nature's plan,
   And none but he!
        — *Robert Burns*

———— • ◆ • ————

We must be as careful to keep friends as to make them.

        — *Lord Avebury*

———— • ◆ • ————

Men know the number of their possessions, although they be very numerous, but of their friends, though but few, they were not only ignorant of the number, but even when they attempted to reckon it to such as asked them, they set aside again some that they have previously counted among their friends; so little did they allow their friends to occupy their thoughts. Yet in comparison with what possession would not a good friend appear far more valuable?

        — *Socrates*

———— • ◆ • ————

If a man does not make new acquaintances as he advances through life, he will soon find himself left alone. A man should keep his friendship in constant repair.

        — *Samuel Johnson*

[35]

You Are My Friend

To wail friends lost
Is not by much so wholesome profitable
As to rejoice at friends but newly found.
— *William Shakespeare*

———— • ◆ • ————

It is delightful to me to go mad over a friend restored to me.

— *Horace*

———— • ◆ • ————

My friend, the brother of my love.
— *Alfred Lord Tennyson*

———— • ◆ • ————

True friends visit us in prosperity, only when invited; but in adversity they come without invitation.
— *Theophrastus*

———— • ◆ • ————

Were I made to prognosticate the future of a man, I would first put my ear to his heart.
— *Alfred Henry Lewis*

———— • ◆ • ————

Life hath no joy like his who fights with Fate
Shoulder to shoulder with a stricken friend.
— *Watts-Dunton*

[36]

Being A Friend

A day for toil, an hour for sport,
But for a friend is life too short.
— *Ralph Waldo Emerson*

——— • ◆ • ———

He sticks through thick and thin—I admire such a man.

— *Abraham Lincoln*

——— • ◆ • ———

To bear a friend's faults is to make them your own.

— *Publilius Syrus*

——— • ◆ • ———

Does it make a man worse than his character's such
As to make his friends love him (as you think) too much?
— *James Russell Lowell*

——— • ◆ • ———

A true friend is forever a friend.

— *McDonald*

——— • ◆ • ———

I had three chairs in my house; one for solitude, two for friendship, three for society.
— *Henry David Thoreau*

[37]

You Are My Friend

He does good to himself, who does good to his friend.

— *Erasmus*

———— • ♦ • ————

Friend-making, everywhere, friend-finding soul,
Fit for the sunshine, so, it followed him.
— *Robert Browning*

———— • ♦ • ————

Never do a wrong thing to make a friend or to keep one.

— *Robert E. Lee*

———— • ♦ • ————

What's the good of money if it ain't to help a friend out with? I believe in friends, I do. Here we go hopping around this little world for a small time, and then that's done. S'pose you ain't got any real friends for the trip? Rotten, I say.

— *Henry Wallace Phillips*

———— • ♦ • ————

This is my friend—through good or ill report
My friend. He who injures him by word or deed,
Were it but the thin film of an idle breath
Clouding the clear glass of a stainless soul,
He injures me.
— *Richard Hovey*

[38]

Being A Friend

Grieve not at doing well to friends
But rather, if thou hast not, grieve.
— *Plautus*

——— • ♦ • ———

The name of friend is common, but faith in friendship is rare.

— *Phaedrus*

——— • ♦ • ———

We may have many acquaintances, but we can
have few friends.

— *Samuel Johnson*

——— • ♦ • ———

Two friends, two bodies with one soul inspired.
— *Alexander Pope*

——— • ♦ • ———

It is not so difficult to sacrifice principle to oblige
a friend as it is to give up one's feeling of superiority
over him.

— *Bruce Henderson*

——— • ♦ • ———

He who looks into the face of a friend beholds, as it
were, a copy of himself.

— *Cicero*

You Are My Friend

Common friendship will admit of division, one may love the beauty of this, the good humor of that person, the liberality of a third, the paternal affection of a fourth, the fraternal love of a fifth, and so on. But this friendship that possesses the whole soul, and there rules and sways with an absolute sovereignty, can admit of no rival.

— *Michael de Montaigne*

———— • ◆ • ————

You have done me friendships infinite and often.
— *Beaumont Fletcher*

———— • ◆ • ————

The happiest moments my heart knows are those in which it is pouring forth its affections to a few esteemed characters.

— *Thomas Jefferson*

———— • ◆ • ————

A true heart admits of but one friendship, as of one love; but in having that friend I have a thousand.
— *William Wycherly*

———— • ◆ • ————

A friend ought to shun no pain, to stand his friend in stead.

— *Richard Edwards*

Being A Friend

So, if I live or die to serve my friend,
'T is for my love—'t is for my friend alone,
And not for any rate that friendship bears
In heaven or on earth.
— *George Eliot*

———— • ♦ • ————

It is no excuse for wrong doing that you do wrong
for the sake of a friend.
— *Cicero*

———— • ♦ • ————

Of all earthly music that which reaches farthest
into heaven is the beating of a loving heart.
— *Henry Ward Beecher*

———— • ♦ • ————

Whene'er we grasp the hands of those
We would have for ever nigh,
The flame of friendship burns and glows
In the warm, frank words "Good-bye."
— *Eliza Cook*

———— • ♦ • ————

The friendship between you and me I will not
compare to a chain; for that the rains might rust, or
the falling tree break.
— *George Bancroft*

[41]

You Are My Friend

Let us be friends, and treat each other like friends.
— *Abraham Lincoln*

——— • ◆ • ———

Who ne'er knew joy but friendship
might divide.
— *Alexander Pope*

——— • ◆ • ———

When a friend asks, there is no to-morrow.
— *Proverb*

——— • ◆ • ———

The solitude of the most sublime idealist is broken
in upon by other people's faces; he sees a look in their
eyes that corresponds to something in his own heart;
there comes a tone in their voice which convicts him
of a startling weakness for his fellow creatures.
— *Robert Louis Stevenson*

——— • ◆ • ———

Oh, the present is too sweet
To go on forever thus!
Who can say what waits for us?
Meeting, greeting, night and day,
Faring each the self-same way—
Still somewhere the path must end—
Reach your hand to me, my friend!
— *James Whitcomb Riley*

Being A Friend

What can be more encouraging than to find the friend who was welcome at one age welcome at another?

— *Robert Louis Stevenson*

———— • ◆ • ————

Of our mixed life two quests are given control:
Food for the body, friendship for the soul.
High as the spirit hovers o'er its flesh
The second quest is free, serene, and fresh.
O sorrow, that so oft the first betrays
This eager searching of celestial ways!
O bitter sorrow that the first can rise
And pluck his soaring brother from the skies!
And there is joy in musing how there can be,
These twain in some lives ruling tranquilly.

— *Arthur Upson*

———— • ◆ • ————

None may charge that I have smiled on him in order to use him, or called him my friend that I might make him do for me the work of a servant.

— *James Lane Allen*

———— • ◆ • ————

The desire to be beloved is ever restless and unsatisfied; but the love that flows out upon others is a perpetual wellspring from on high.

— *Lydia Maria Child*

You Are My Friend

Nothing is more friendly to a man than a friend in need.
— *Plautus*

———— • ♦ • ————

Judge not thy friend until thou standest in his place.
— *Rabbi Hillel*

———— • ♦ • ————

What we commonly call friends and friendships are nothing but acquaintance and connection, contracted either by accident or upon some design, by means of which there happens some little intercourse betwixt our souls: but, in the friendship I speak of, they mingle and melt into one piece, with so universal a mixture that there is left no more sign of the seam by which they were first conjoined.
— *Michael de Montaigne*

———— • ♦ • ————

I weigh my friend's affection with mine own.
— *William Shakespeare*

———— • ♦ • ————

A fellow feeling makes one wondrous kind.
— *David Garrick*

[44]

Being A Friend

Friendship is the simple reflection of souls by each other.

— *William Alger*

——— • ♦ • ———

Greater love hath no man than this, that a man lay down his life for his friends.

— *Book of John*

——— • ♦ • ———

Absent or present, still to thee
My friend, what magic spells belong.
— *Lord Byron*

——— • ♦ • ———

What do we live for if not to make life less difficult to each other.

— *George Eliot*

——— • ♦ • ———

Two may talk under the same roof for may years, yet never really meet; and two others at first speech are old friends.

— *Mary Catherwood*

You Are My Friend

Animals are such agreeable friends—they ask no questions, they pass no criticisms.
— *George Eliot*

———— • ◆ • ————

Statesman, yet friend to truth! of soul serene,
   In action faithful, and in honor clear;
   Who broke no promise, served no private end,
Who gained no title, and who lost no friend.
— *Alexander Pope*

———— • ◆ • ————

Winter, spring, summer or fall
All you have to do is call
And I'll be there,
You've got a friend.
— *Carole King*

5

BEING BEFRIENDED

I don't readily forget old friends, nor easily stop loving anybody I have ever loved. However, I learned long ago not to expect more than three people to care for me at a time—maybe I'm extravagant in saying three.

— *James Russell Lowell*

———— • ◆ • ————

The parable of Pythagoras is dark, but true, "Cor ne edito"—eat not the heart. Certainly, if a man would give it a hard phrase, those that want friends to open themselves unto are cannibals of their own hearts.

— *Francis Bacon*

———— • ◆ • ————

Much as worthy friends add to the happiness and value of life, we must in the main depend upon ourselves, and every one is his own best friend, or worst enemy.

— *Lord Avebury*

[47]

You Are My Friend

Ah, friends! before my listening ear lies low,
While I can hear and understand, bestow
    That gentle treatment and fond love, I pray.
    The luster of whose late, though radiant ray
Would gild my grave with mocking light, I know,
If I should die.

— Ella Wheeler Wilcox

———— • ♦ • ————

Happy is he who wins friends in early life by true
affinities. He multiplies himself; he has more hands
and feet than his own, and other fortresses to flee into
when his own are dismantled by evil fortune, and
other hearts to throb with his joy.

— Theodore Munger

———— • ♦ • ————

It is strange thing to behold what gross errors and
extreme absurdities many (especially of the greater
sort) do commit for the want of a friend to tell them of
them.

— Francis Bacon

———— • ♦ • ————

The greatest happiness of life is the conviction
that we are loved, loved for ourselves, or rather loved
in spite of ourselves.

— Victor Hugo

[48]

Being Befriended

Companions I have enough, friends few.
— *Alexander Pope*

——— • ◆ • ———

Oh! as we prove the life-boat, so we often prove a friend;
And those who promist least of all, are truest in the end.
No figure-head of gold and red may mark them as they go;
But how their honest planks will stand when trouble-tempests
  blow.
They may not dance around us on the broad and sunlit tide,
But 'twixt the gale and dark lee-shore we find them close
  beside.
A cheer, then, for the noble breast that fears not danger's
  post:
And, like the life-boat, proves a friend, when friends are wanted
  most.

— *Eliza Cook*

——— • ◆ • ———

Anacharsis coming to Athens, knocked at Solon's door, and told him that he, being a stranger, was come to be his guest, and contract a friendship with him; and Solon replying, "It is better to make friends at home," Anacharsis replied, "Then you that are at home make friendship with me."

— *Plutarch*

——— • ◆ • ———

Above our life we love a faithful friend.
— *Marlowe*

[49]

You Are My Friend

There is more to do than one can do alone, and an unfriended life will be poor and meager.
— *Theodore Munger*

———— • ◆ • ————

A pleasant companion on the way is as good as a carriage.
— *Publilius Syrus*

———— • ◆ • ————

A friend is dearer than the light of heaven; for it would be better for us that the sun were extinguished, than that we should be without friends.
— *Saint John Chrysostom*

———— • ◆ • ————

If, as a mere matter of strength and resource, I were to face life with the choice of either a fortune or friends, I would choose the latter as more helpful.
— *Theodore Munger*

———— • ◆ • ————

Large was his bounty, and his soul serene,
   Heaven did a recompense as largely send;
He gave to Misery all he had, a tear;
   He gained from Heaven ('t was all he wished) a friend.
— *Thomas Gray*

[50]

Being Befriended

I account more strength in a true heart than in a walled city.

— John Lyle

———— • ◆ • ————

We were friends from the first moment. Sincere attachments usually begin at the beginning.

— Joseph Jefferson

———— • ◆ • ————

One faithful friend is enough for a man's self; 't is much to meet with such an one.

— Jean de la Bruyère

———— • ◆ • ————

What is a friend? One who supports you and comforts you, while others do not.

— Samuel Johnson

———— • ◆ • ————

A friend is not so soon gotten as lost.

— Porter

———— • ◆ • ————

Nothing is dearer to a man than a serviceable friend.

— Plautus

[51]

You Are My Friend

Friendship enhances the luster of prosperity and by dividing and sharing adversity lessens its burden.
— *Cicero*

———— • ♦ • ————

I'm very lonely now, Mary,
   For the poor make no new friends;
But oh, they love the better still
   The few our Father sends!
— *Lady Dufferin*

———— • ♦ • ————

Be a friend; the rest will follow.
— *Dickerson*

———— • ♦ • ————

We attract hearts by the qualities we display; we retain them by the qualities we possess.
— *Suard*

———— • ♦ • ————

To be rich in friends is to be poor in nothing.
— *Lilian Whiting*

———— • ♦ • ————

My dearest meed, a friend's esteem and praise.
— *Robert Burns*

[52]

Being Befriended

He does nothing who consoles a despairing man with his words; he is a friend who in a difficulty helps by deeds, where there is need of deeds.

— *Plautus*

———— • ♦ • ————

But other loads than this his own
One man is not well made to bear.
Besides, to each are his own friends,
To mourn with him, and show him care.

— *Matthew Arnold*

———— • ♦ • ————

That faithful friendship which never changes, and which will accompany you with its calm light through the whole of life.

— *Frederica Bremer*

———— • ♦ • ————

Friendship, like the immortality of the soul, is too good to be believed.

— *Ralph Waldo Emerson*

———— • ♦ • ————

A companion on the way is better than money in the purse.

— *French Proverb*

[53]

You Are My Friend

Sweet the help
Of one we have helped.
— *Elizabeth Browning*

———— • ◆ • ————

His honest, sonsie, baws'nt face
Aye got him friends in ilka place.
— *Robert Burns*

———— • ◆ • ————

There is as yet no culture, no method of progress known to men, that is so rich and complete as that which is ministered by a truly great friendship.
— *Phillips Brooks*

———— • ◆ • ————

I have known one who used to beg of holy men to pray, first for his friend and then for himself.
— *Saint John Chrysostom*

———— • ◆ • ————

Who takes a fool to be his friend
Will stay a fool until the end.
— *John Holden*

———— • ◆ • ————

O, be my friend, and teach me to be thine.
— *Ralph Waldo Emerson*

[54]

Being Befriended

Friendship knows nothing of bankrupt sentiment and collapsed joys; love, after giving more than it has, ends by giving less than it receives.

— *Honoré de Balzac*

———— • ♦ • ————

It is sublime to feel and say of another, I need never meet, or speak or write to him; we need not reinforce ourselves or send tokens of remembrance; I rely on him as on myself; if he did thus and thus, I know it was right.

— *Ralph Waldo Emerson*

———— • ♦ • ————

And thou, my friend, whose gentle love
Yet thrills my bosom's chords,
How much thy friendship was above
Description's power of words.
— *Lord Byron*

———— • ♦ • ————

We talk of taxes and I call you friend.
— *Edna St. Vincent Millay*

———— • ♦ • ————

I'm very lonely now—for the poor make no new friends.

— *Lady Montagu*

You Are My Friend

I believe that more breaches of friendship and love have been created, and more hatred cemented by needless criticism than by any one other thing.
— *Sir Arthur Helps*

———— • ♦ • ————

To act the part of a true friend requires more conscientious feeling than to fill with credit and complacency any other station or capacity in life.
— *Sarah Ellis*

6
THE ADVICE OF
FRIENDS

Advice can hardly come from any other than a friend when the question involves grave issues. A stranger is not sufficiently interested, a relative is blinded by excess of love, but a friend's advice is tempered by affection, while it is not over-ruled by the imperativeness of natural instinct. There is much wisdom in the every-day words "As a friend I advise you," for no other can advise so well.

— *Theodore Munger*

———— • ◆ • ————

Too true to flatter, and too kind to sneer,
And only just when seemingly severe;
So gently blending courtesy and art,
That wisdom's lips seemed borrowing friendship's heart.
— *Oliver Wendell Holmes*

———— • ◆ • ————

Softening harsh words in friendship's gentle tone.
— *Percy Bysshe Shelley*

You Are My Friend

Animals are such agreeable friends—they ask no questions, they pass no criticisms.

— *George Eliot*

———— • ◆ • ————

Friendship must be something else than a society for mutual improvement—indeed, it must only be that by the way, and to some extent unconsciously.

— *Robert Louis Stevenson*

———— • ◆ • ————

If it is abuse, why, one is always sure to hear it from one damned good-natured friend or another.

— *Richard Sheridan*

———— • ◆ • ————

Ointment and perfume rejoice the heart: so doth the sweetness of a man's friend by hearty counsel.

— *Proverbs*

———— • ◆ • ————

Heraclitus saith well, in one of his enigmas, "Dry light is ever the best." And certain it is that the light that a man receiveth by counsel from another is drier and purer than that which cometh from his own understanding and judgment which is ever infused and drenched in his affections and customs.

— *Francis Bacon*

[58]

The Advice of Friends

You seldom need wait for the written life of a man to hear about his weaknesses, or what are supposed to be such, if you know his intimate friends or meet him in company with them.

— Sir Arthur Helps

——— • ◆ • ———

The best preservatve to keep the mind in health is the faithful admonition of a friend.

— Francis Bacon

——— • ◆ • ———

Admonish your friends in private; praise them in public.

— Publilius Syrus

——— • ◆ • ———

There is no man so friendless but what he can find a friend sincere enough to tell him disagreeable truths.

— Edward Bulwer Lytton

——— • ◆ • ———

Friends require to be advised and reproved, and such treatment, when it is kindly, should be taken in a friendly spirit.

— Cicero

[59]

You Are My Friend

A friend advises by his whole behavior, and never condescends to particulars. Another chides away a fault, he loves it away. While he sees the other's error he is silently conscious of it, and only the more loves truth itself, and assists his friend in loving it, till the fault is expelled and gently extinguished.

— *Henry David Thoreau*

———— • ◆ • ————

A friend's frown is better than a fool's smile.

— *Proverb*

———— • ◆ • ————

Before giving advice we must have secured its acceptance, rather, have made it desired.

— *Amiel's Journal*

———— • ◆ • ————

It is well and right, indeed to be courteous and considerate to every one with whom we are brought into contact, but to choose them as real friends is another matter.

— *Lord Avebury*

———— • ◆ • ————

I speak to thee in Friendship's name.

—*Thomas Moore*

The Advice of Friends

He that gives advice to his friend and exacts obedience to it, does not the kindness and ingenuity of a friend, but the office and pertness of a shcoolmaster.

— *Jeremy Taylor*

——— • ♦ • ———

Friendship e'er totters on the brink,
With friends who say just what they think;
They end, who give advice unsought,
In saying what they never thought.
— *Christopher Bannister*

——— • ♦ • ———

There is as much difference between the counsel that a friend giveth and that a man giveth himself as there is between the counsel of a friend and a flatterer; for there is no such flatterer as a man's self, and there is no such remedy against flattery of a man's self as the liberty of a friend.

— *Francis Bacon*

——— • ♦ • ———

I am speaking now of the highest duty we owe our friends, the nobleness, goodness, pure and incorrupt ... If we let our friends become cold and selfish and exacting without a remonstrance, we are no true lover, no true friend.

— *Harriet Beecher Stowe*

[61]

7

FRIENDS AND ENEMIES

God preserve me from my friends; from my enemies I will preserve myself.

— *Italian Proverb*

———— • ♦ • ————

When fails our dearest friend,
There may be refuge with our direst foe.
— *James S. Knowles*

———— • ♦ • ————

It is always safe to learn, even from our enemies; seldom safe to venture to instruct even our friends.
— *Caleb C. Colton*

———— • ♦ • ————

Give me the avowed, the erect, the manly foe;
Bold I can meet, perhaps may turn his blow;
But of all plagues, good Heaven, thy wrath can send,
Save, save, oh! save me from the Candid Friend!
— *George Channing*

[63]

You Are My Friend

Let us not talk ill of our enemies. They only never deceive us.

— *Arsene Houssaye*

——— • ◆ • ———

An open foe may prove a curse,
But a pretended friend is worse.
— *John Gay*

——— • ◆ • ———

Ye have heard that it hath been said, Thou shalt love thy neighbor and hate thine enemy. But I say unto you, Love your enemies, bless them that curse you, do good to them that hate you, and pray for them which despitefully use you, and persecute you; that you may be the children of your Father which is in heaven: for He maketh His sun to rise on the evil and on the good, and sendeth rain on the just and on the unjust. For if ye love them which love you, what reward have ye? Do not even the publicans the same? And if ye salute your brethren only, what do ye more than others? Do not even the publicans so?

— *Book of Matthew*

——— • ◆ • ———

If thine enemy hunger, feed him; if he thirst, give him drink: for in so doing thou shalt heap coals of fire on his head.

— *Romans II*

[64]

Friends and Enemies

A man who does not love sincerely sets his face against the distinguishing mark between a friend and a flatterer.

— Alain René Lesago

———— • ◆ • ————

Faithful are the wounds of a friend, but the kisses of an enemy are deceitful.

— Proverbs

———— • ◆ • ————

Love springs to love, and knows at once his friends.
The man who hates must cast contentment forth;
Who has not worth or friends is nothing worth.

— Alain Chartier

———— • ◆ • ————

Unfortunately, while there are few great friends, there is no little enemy.

— Lord Avebury

———— • ◆ • ————

Fellowship is heaven, and lack of fellowship is hell; fellowship is life, and lack of fellowship is death; and the deeds that ye do upon earth, it is for fellowship's sake that ye do them.

— William Morris

You Are My Friend

A foe to God was ne'er true friend to man,
Some sinister intent taints all he does.
— *Edward Young*

——— • ♦ • ———

Dear is my friend,—yet from my foe as from my friend, comes
  good;
My friend shows what I can do, and my foe what I should.
— *Johann Schiller*

——— • ♦ • ———

The greatest enmity is better than uncertain
friendship.

— *Hindoo Proverb*

——— • ♦ • ———

It is better to have bitter foes than friends too
sweet.

— *Cato*

——— • ♦ • ———

It is a difficult task to have all men for your friends:
it is sufficient not to have enemies.

— *Seneca*

——— • ♦ • ———

A bitter heart that bides its time and bites.
— *Robert Browning*

Friends and Enemies

Better to have a loving friend
Than ten admiring foes.
— *George Macdonald*

———— • ♦ • ————

He will never have true friends who is afraid of making enemies.

— *William Hazlitt*

———— • ♦ • ————

Better friends at a distance than neighbors and enemies.

— *Italian Proverb*

———— • ♦ • ————

One enemy can do more hurt than ten friends can do good.

— *Jonathan Swift*

———— • ♦ • ————

Trust not yourself; but your defects to know,
Make use of every friend—and every foe.
— *Alexander Pope*

———— • ♦ • ————

Friends are as dangerous as enemies.

— *De Quincy*

[67]

You Are My Friend

The world is large when its weary leagues two loving hearts
    divide;
But the world is small when your enemy is loose on the other
    side.

— John Boyle O'Reilly

———— • ♦ • ————

Invite the man that loves thee to a feast, but let
alone thine enemy.

— Hesiod

———— • ♦ • ————

Flatterers look like friends, as wolves like dogs.
— George Chapman

———— • ♦ • ————

No enemy
Is half so fatal as a friend estranged.
— Davidson

———— • ♦ • ————

It has been said that it is wise always to treat a
friend remembering that he may become an enemy,
and an enemy remembering that he may become a
friend; and whate'er may be thought of the first part of
the adage, there is certainly much wisdom in the
latter.

— Lord Avebury

[68]

Friends and Enemies

I wish my deadly foe no worse
Than want of friends, and empty purse.
— *Nicholas Breton*

——— • ♦ • ———

Our enmities mortal, our friendships eternal.
— *Cicero*

——— • ♦ • ———

Angry friendship is sometimes as bad as calm enmity.
— *Edmund Burke*

——— • ♦ • ———

An ignorant friend is dangerous e'er;
A foe who is wise I greatly prefer.
— *La Fontaine*

——— • ♦ • ———

An thou wilt be friends, be friends: an thou wilt not, why, then be enemies.
— *William Shakespeare*

——— • ♦ • ———

Here's a sigh to those who love me,
    And a smile to those who hate;
And, whatever sky's above me,
    Here's a heart for every fate.
— *Lord Byron*

[69]

You Are My Friend

A friend cannot be known in prosperity, and an enemy cannot be hidden in adversity.
— *Theophrastus*

———— • ◆ • ————

Better new friend than old foe.
—*Herbert Spenser*

———— • ◆ • ————

Foes sometimes befriend us more, our blacker deeds objecting,
Than th' obsequious bosom guest, with false respect affecting,
Friendship is the Glass of Truth, our hidden stains detecting.
— *Thomas Campion*

———— • ◆ • ————

Greatly his foes he dreads, but more his friends;
He hurts me most who lavishly commends.
— *Charles Churchill*

———— • ◆ • ————

Spare to us our friends, soften to us our enemies.
— *Robert Louis Stevenson*

———— • ◆ • ————

Some great misfortune to portend,
No enemy can match a friend.
— *Jonathan Swift*

[70]

Friends and Enemies

The man who hates must cast contentment forth.
— *Alain Chartier*

————— • ♦ • —————

Mutual love brings mutual delight,—
Brings beauty, life,—for love is life, hate death.
— *Richard Dana*

————— • ♦ • —————

Many people seem to take more pains and more
pleasure in making enemies than in making friends.
— *Lord Avebury*

————— • ♦ • —————

Disloyalty, that hatefullest of sins,
Still teaches us where loyalty begins.
— *John Holden*

————— • ♦ • —————

Though lions to their enemies they were lambs to
their friends.

— *Benjamin Disraeli*

————— • ♦ • —————

His must be a very wretched fortune who has no
enemy.

— *Publilius Syrus*

You Are My Friend

He who has a thousand friends,
  Has not a friend to spare,
And he who has one enemy
  Will meet him everywhere.
                              — *Ali Ben Abu Taheb*

——— • ◆ • ———

Friendly counsel cuts off many foes.
                              — *William Shakespeare*

——— • ◆ • ———

I force no friend, I fear no foe.
                              — *Lord Byron*

——— • ◆ • ———

Happy long life with honor at the close,
Friends' painless tears, the softened thought of foes.
                              — *James Russell Lowell*

——— • ◆ • ———

Do good to thy friend to keep him, to thy enemy to gain him.
                              — *Benjamin Franklin*

——— • ◆ • ———

The richer your friends the more they will cost you.
                              — *Elisabeth Marbury*

Friends and Enemies

Before the flowers of friendship faded friendship faded.

— *Gertrude Stein*

[73]

8

MEN AND WOMEN FRIENDS

It is a wonderful advantage to a man, in every pursuit or avocation, to secure an adviser in a sensible woman. In woman there is at once a subtle delicacy of tact, and a plain soundness of judgment, which are rarely combined to an equal degree in man. A woman, if she be really your friend, will have a sensitive regard for your character, honor, repute. She will seldom counsel you to do a shabby thing; for a woman friend desires to be proud of you. At the same time her constitutional timidity makes her more cautious than your male friend. She, therefore, seldom counsels you to do an imprudent thing. A man's best female friend is a wife of good sense and good heart, whom he loves, and who loves him. If he have that, he need not seek elsewhere. but supposing the man be without such a helpmate, female friendship he must have, or his intellect will be without a garden, and there will be many an unheeded gap even in its strongest fence.

— *Edward Bulwer Lytton*

You Are My Friend

> Men have known
> No fairer friendship than the fair have shown.
> — *William Cowper*

———— • ◆ • ————

It is great happiness to form a sincere friendship with a woman.

— *Sydney Smith*

———— • ◆ • ————

The friendship of a man is often a support; that of a woman is always a consolation.

— *Rochepèdre*

———— • ◆ • ————

A woman's love is often a misfortune; her friendship is always a boon.

— *Louis Mézières*

———— • ◆ • ————

Women sometimes deceive the lover, never the friend.

— *Mercier*

———— • ◆ • ————

There is no friendship equal to that of a woman.
— *William Alger*

[76]

Men and Women Friends

A man should not repudiate the friendship of a woman, because it may lead to harm: he should cherish the friendship and beware of the harm.

— William Alger

———— • ♦ • ————

Curious that this topic of friendship is so especially alluring to a man and woman between whom friendship is impossible.

— Margaret Deland

———— • ♦ • ————

Friendship is no respecter of sex, and perhaps it is more rare between the sexes than between two of the same sex.

— Henry David Thoreau

———— • ♦ • ————

Friendship that begins between a man and a woman will soon change its name.

— Author Unknown

———— • ♦ • ————

Admiration and love are like being intoxicated with champagne; judgment and friendship like being enlivened.

— Samuel Johnson

You Are My Friend

A woman's friendship borders more closely on love than a man's.

— *Samuel Taylor Coleridge*

——— • ♦ • ———

Women need friendship more than men, because they are less self-sufficing.

— *William Alger*

——— • ♦ • ———

Female friendship, indeed, is to a man the bulwark, sweetener, ornament, of his existence. To his mental culture it is invaluable: without it all his knowledge of books will never give him knowledge of the world.

— *Michael de Montaigne*

——— • ♦ • ———

The only true and firm friendship is that between man and woman, because it is the only one free from all possible competition.

— *Auguste Comte*

——— • ♦ • ———

What distinguishes this platonic affection from ordinary friendship, is, that the magic of imagination, with a religious emphasis is in it.

— *William Alger*

Men and Women Friends

Love will obtain and possess; friendship makes
sacrifices, but asks nothing.

— Emanuel von Geibel

——— • ◆ • ———

One should choose for a wife only such a woman
as he would choose for a friend, were she a man.

— Joseph Joubert

——— • ◆ • ———

I have always laid it down as a maxim, and found it
justified by experience, that a man and a woman make
far better friendships than can exist between two of
the same sex; but with this condition, that they never
have made, or are to make, love with each other.

— Lord Byron

——— • ◆ • ———

The reason why so few women are touched by
friendship is that they find it dull when they have
experienced love.

— Francois de la Rochefoucauld

——— • ◆ • ———

The men are the occasion the women do not love
each other.

— Jean de la Bruyére

You Are My Friend

A woman friend! He that believes that weakness
Steers in a stormy night without a compass.

— Fletcher

———— • ♦ • ————

To speak the truth, I never yet knew a tolerable
woman to be fond of her sex.

— Jonathan Swift

———— • ♦ • ————

Two women faster welded in one love
Than pairs of wedlock

— Alfred Lord Tennyson

———— • ♦ • ————

The enduring elegance of female friendship.

— Samuel Johnson

———— • ♦ • ————

No friendship is so cordial or so delicious as that
of girl for girl.

— John Savage Landor

———— • ♦ • ————

Friendship between two women is always a plot
against each other.

— Alphonse Karr

Men and Women Friends

On all her days let health and peace attend,
May she ne'er want, nor ever lose, a friend.
— *George Lyttleton*

———— • ♦ • ————

It is the fashion to deride female friendship, to look with scorn on those who profess it. There is always to me a doubt of the warmth, the strength, the purity of her feelings, when a girl merges into womanhood looking down on female friendship as romance and folly.

— *Grace Aguilar*

———— • ♦ • ————

The friendships of women are much more common than those of men; but rarely or never, so firm, so just, or so enduring.

— *Dinah Muloch*

———— • ♦ • ————

Women have no worse enemies than women.
— *Jean Duclos*

———— • ♦ • ————

Friendships of women are cushions wherein they stick their pins.

— *Author Unknown*

[81]

You Are My Friend

If you have derived your ideas on the subject from books only, it is possible that you have not the faintest conception what a good, honest, and substantial thing a young woman's friendship really is.

— *Blanche Howard*

———— • ◆ • ————

Women are armed with microscopes to see all the little defects and dissimilarities which can irritate and injure their friendships.

— *William Alger*

———— • ◆ • ————

And one shall give, perchance hath given,
   What only is not love.
Friendship, oh, such as saints in heaven
   Rain on us from above.

— *Felicia Hemans*

———— • ◆ • ————

Men have known no fairer friendship than the fair have shown.

— *William Alger*

———— • ◆ • ————

A woman's friendship is, as a rule, the legacy of love or the alms of indifference.

— *Author Unknown*

[82]

Men and Women Friends

What woman who possessed a ring conferring invisibility on its wearer, would dare to put it on and move about among—her friends.

— *William Alger*

———— • ◆ • ————

My true friends have always given me, that supreme proof of devotion, a spontaneous aversion for the man I loved.

— *Colette*

———— • ◆ • ————

Women are naturally less selfish and more sympathetic than men. They have more affection to bestow, greater need of sympathy, and therefore are more sure, in the absence of love, to seek friendship.

— *William Alger*

9
FRIENDS AND
RELATIONS

Friendship, in its full sense, has precedence of kinship in this particular that the good will may be taken away from kinship, not from friendship, for when good will is removed, friendship loses its name, while that of kinship remains.

— *Cicero*

———— • ◆ • ————

None such true friends, none so sweet life,
As that between the man and wife.
— *Thomas Campion*

———— • ◆ • ————

Whatever the degree of kinship, without friendship added to it, it becomes worse than foolishness. Conceive of a happy marriage, a proud parent, a loving child, without a firm foundation of friendship—it is impossible!

— *Robert L. Lorimer*

[85]

You Are My Friend

Better one true friend than a host of kinsfolk.
— *Italian Proverb*

———— • ♦ • ————

Happy the man who has persuaded a maiden into loving wifehood; thrice happy the husband who has persuaded his wife into a firm friendship!
— *Frances F. Graves*

———— • ♦ • ————

Friends agree best at a distance. By friends here is meant relations.
— *Scots Proverb*

———— • ♦ • ————

A child may be an affliction, or a parent a misfortune; but a friend is a man's own fault.
— *George Ade*

———— • ♦ • ————

Oh, how sweet a name, and how full of tenderness, is that of brother.
— *Eugénie de Guérin*

———— • ♦ • ————

A good friend is better than a near relation.
— *Old Proverb*

Friends and Relations

Though human, thou didst not decieve me,
  Though woman, thou didst not forsake;
Though loved, thou forborest to grieve me,
  Though slandered, thou never couldst shake,
Though trusted, thou didst not disclaim me,
  Though parted, it was not to fly,
Though watchful, 't was not to defame me,
  Nor mute, that the world might belie.

— Lord Byron

——— • ◆ • ———

It is chance that makes brothers, but hearts that make friends.

— Author Unknown

——— • ◆ • ———

Between persons perpetually in one another's company dislike or affection increases daily.

— Honoré de Balzac

——— • ◆ • ———

Friendship excels relationship.

— Cicero

——— • ◆ • ———

To me she was not only the companion of my studies, but the sweetener of my toils.

— William Wirt

[87]

You Are My Friend

I have ever sought a friendship so strong and earnest that only death could break it; a happiness which I had in my brother.

— *Eugénie de Guérin*

——— • ♦ • ———

I hope I do not break the fifth commandment, if I conceive I may love my friend before the nearest of my blood.

— *Sir Thomas Browne*

——— • ♦ • ———

My sister, my sweet sister! if a name
Dearer and purer were, it should be thine.

— *Lord Byron*

——— • ♦ • ———

A friend loveth at all times, and a brother is born for adversity.

— *Proverbs*

——— • ♦ • ———

There is in friendship something of all relations, and something above them all. It is the golden thread that ties the hearts of all the world.

— *John Evelyn*

Friends and Relations

Thou to me didst ever show
Kindest affection; and would oft-times lend
An ear to the desponding love-sick lay,
Weeping my sorrows with me, who repay
but ill the mighty debt of love I owe,
Mary, to thee, my sister and my friend.
— *Charles Lamb*

———— • ♦ • ————

A man can speak to his son but as a father, to his wife but as a husband; to his enemy but upon terms; whereas a friend may speak as the case requires, and not as it sorteth with the person.

— *Francis Bacon*

10
OLD FRIENDS

Ask where a man's glory first begins and ends.
And say my glory was I has such friends.
                              — *W.B. Yeats*

———— • ♦ • ————

We just shake hands at meeting
    With many that come nigh;
We nod the head in greeting
    To many that go by.
But welcome through the gateway
    Our few old friends and true;
Then hearts leap up and straightway
    There's open house for you,
        Old Friends,
    There's open house for you!
                              — *Gerald Massey*

———— • ♦ • ————

Dag gone it 'Ras! they haint no friend,
It 'pears like, left to comprehend
Sich things as these but you, and see
How dratted sweet they air to me!
    And so, Ras Wilson, stop and shake
    A paw, fer old acquaintance sake!
                              — *James Whitcomb Riley*

[91]

You Are My Friend

Time draweth wrinkles in a fair face, but addeth fresh colors to a fast friend.

— John Lyle

———— • ◆ • ————

The best mirror is an old friend.

— Proverb

———— • ◆ • ————

We have been friends together
In sunshine and in shade.
— Caroline Norton

———— • ◆ • ————

How unspeakably the lengthening of memories in common endears our old friends!

— George Eliot

———— • ◆ • ————

How much the best of a man's friend is his oldest friend.

— Plautus

———— • ◆ • ————

Do not trouble yourself much to get new things, whether clothes or friends. Turn the old; return to them.

— Henry David Thoreau

Old Friends

Is not old wine wholesomest, old pippins tooth-some, old wood burns brightest, old linen wash whitest? Old soldiers are surest, and old lovers are soundest.

— *John Webster*

———— • ◆ • ————

Friends we have, if we have merited them. Those of our earliest years stand nearest in our affections.

— *Thomas Jefferson*

———— • ◆ • ————

Old friends are best. King James used to call for his old shoes; they were easiest for his feet.

— *John Selden*

———— • ◆ • ————

Each year to ancient friendship adds a ring,
As to an oak, and precious more and more,
Without deservingness or help of ours,
They grow, and, silent, wider spread, each year,
Their unbought ring of shelter or of shade.

— *James Russell Lowell*

———— • ◆ • ————

When old age comes, that man is poor indeed—in heart—compared with what he might have been, if he has loved no life-long friend.

— *Perry Marshall*

[93]

You Are My Friend

Old friends burn dim, like lamps in noisome air;
Love them for what they are; nor love them less,
Because to thee they are not what they were.
— *Samuel Taylor Coleridge*

——— • ◆ • ———

It is easy to say how we love new friends, and what we think of them, but words can never trace out all the fibers that knit us to the old.
— *George Eliot*

——— • ◆ • ———

Of a sudden at a well-known corner,
In the densest throng,
Unexpected at the very moment
As an April robin's gush of song,
Some one smiles; and there's the perfect comrade
I have missed so long.
— *Bliss Carman*

——— • ◆ • ———

Change, Care, nor Time while life endure,
Shall spoil our ancient friendship sure.
— *Andrew Lang*

——— • ◆ • ———

A friendship counting nearly forty years is the finest kind of shade-tree I know.
— *James Russell Lowell*

[94]

Old Friends

An old friend is like old wine, which, when a man hath drunk, he doth not desire new, because he saith "the old is better".

— *Jeremy Taylor*

———— • ♦ • ————

The place where two friends met is sacred to them all through their friendship, all the more sacred as their friendship deepens and grows old.

— *Phillips Brooks*

———— • ♦ • ————

The older a friendship is the more precious it should be, as is the case with wines that will bear keeping.

— *Cicero*

———— • ♦ • ————

I find friendship to be like wine, raw when new, ripened with age, the true old man's milk and restorative cordial.

— *Thomas Jefferson*

———— • ♦ • ————

Friendship is the shadow of the evening, which strengthens with the setting sun of life.

— *La Fontaine*

You Are My Friend

Alonso of Aragon was wont to say in commendation of age, that age appears to be best in four things, old wood best to burn, old wine to drink, old friends to trust, and old authors to read.

— *Francis Bacon*

——— • ◆ • ———

Old books, old wine, old Nankin blue,
    All things, in short, to which belong
    The charm, the grace that Time makes strong,
All things I prize but (entre nous)
    Old friends are best.

—*Austin Dobson*

——— • ◆ • ———

For forty years and better you have been a friend to me,
Through days of sore afflictions and dire adversity,
You allus had a kind word of counsul to impart,
Which was like a healin' 'intment to the sorrow of my hart.

Ways was devius, William Leachman, that me and you has
    past;
But as I found you true at first, I find you true at last;
And, now the time's a comin' mighty nigh our journey's end,
I want to throw wide open all my soul to you, my friend.

— *James Whitcomb Riley*

——— • ◆ • ———

To me, fair friend, you never can be old,
For as you were when first your eye I ey'd,
Such seems your beauty still.

— *William Shakespeare*

[96]

Old Friends

Should auld acquaintance be forgot,
   And never brought to mind?
Should auld acquaintance be forgot
   And days o'lang syne?
For auld lang syne, my dear,
   For auld lang syne,
We'll take a cup o' kindness yet,
   For auld lang syne.

— *Robert Burns*

———— • ◆ • ————

Old friends are the greatest blessings of one's
latter years. Half a word conveys one's meaning. They
have memory of the same events, and have the same
mode of thinking.

— *Horace Walpole*

———— • ◆ • ————

But what binds us friend to friend,
But that soul with soul can blend?
Soul-like were those hours of yore;
Let us walk in soul once more.

— *Ludwig Uhland*

———— • ◆ • ————

A friend may be often found and lost, but an old
friend can never be found, and nature has provided
that he cannot be easily lost.

— *Samuel Johnson*

[97]

You Are My Friend

What an ocean is life! and how our barks get separated in beating through it! One of the greatest comforts of the retirement to which I shall soon withdraw, will be its rejoining me to my earliest and best friends, and acquaintances.

— *Thomas Jefferson*

———— • ◆ • ————

To grow old with you; when the days grow sere
To have you by me, making time appear
   Our willing servant; at an age awry
   Laughing and jesting as in times gone by;
Recalling youth, O friend ere youth was near,
Has left the sweeter each advancing year.
Still is earth green, and skies are ever clear
   That listen to my happy heart's fond cry
     To grow old with you!

And how old joys return and linger here
In the retelling, how quickly dries the tear
   You smile upon, how quick the new griefs fly!
   So, when fulfillment come, why, then shall I
Smile at my granted wish—how should I fear?—
     To grow old with you.

— *Wallace Rice*

———— • ◆ • ————

A friend may be often found and lost, but an old friend can never be found, and nature has provided that he cannot be easily lost.

— *Samuel Johnson*

[98]

Old Friends

When you have spent your boyhood and played your youthful pranks with a comrade, the sympathy between you and him has something sacred about it; his voice, his glance, stir certain chords in your heart that only vibrate under the memories he brings back.

— *Honoré de Balzac*

———— • ◆ • ————

There muse I of old times, old hopes, old friends.
Old friends! The writing of those words has borne
My fancy backward to the gracious past,
The generous past, when all was possible,
For all was then untried; the years between
Have taught some sweet, some bitter lessons, none
Wiser than this,—to spend in all things else,
But of old friends to be most miserly.

— *James Russell Lowell*

11
FRIENDSHIPS
REMEMBERED

It is a difficult thing to replace true friends.

— *Seneca*

—— • ♦ • ——

Friends are lost by calling often and calling seldom.

— *Proverb*

—— • ♦ • ——

Freeze, freeze, thou bitter sky,
That dost not bite so nigh
  As benefits forgot:
Though thou the waters warp,
Thy sting is not so sharp
  As friend remembered not.
— *William Shakespeare*

—— • ♦ • ——

It is a mere and miserable solitude to want true friends, without which the world is but a wilderness.

— *Francis Bacon*

[101]

You Are My Friend

All are not friends that speak us fair.
— *Proverb*

——— • ◆ • ———

Friendship is a vase which, when it is flawed by heat of violence or accident, may as well be broken at once; it can never be trusted again.
— *Walter Savage Landor*

——— • ◆ • ———

The wretched have no friends.
— *John Dryden*

——— • ◆ • ———

Near friends, falling out, never reunite cordially.
— *Thomas Jefferson*

——— • ◆ • ———

The swallows art at hand in the summer time, but in cold weather they are driven away. So false friends are at hand in life's clear weather; but as soon as they see the winter of fortune, they all fly away.
— *Cicero*

——— • ◆ • ———

A little love has destroyed many a great friendship.
— *Eva Trezevant*

Friendships Remembered

Alas! how light a cause may move
Dissension between two hearts that love!
Hearts that the world in vain had tried,
And sorrow but more closely tied;
That stood the storm when waves were rough,
Yet in a sunny hour fell off,
Like ships that have gone down at sea,
When heaven was all tranquility.
— *Thomas Moore*

———— • ♦ • ————

Broken friendship may be soldered, but never made sound.
— *Spanish Proverb*

———— • ♦ • ————

Who finds himself without friends is like a body without a soul.
— *Italian Proverb*

———— • ♦ • ————

Friendship, take heed; if woman interfere,
Be sure the hour of thy destruction's near,
— *Sir John Vanbrugh*

———— • ♦ • ————

For I am alone, of all my friends, my own friend.
— *Apollodorus*

[103]

You Are My Friend

And such the change the heart displays,
So frail is early friendship's reign,
A month's brief lapse, perhaps a day's
Will view thy mind estranged again.
— *Lord Byron*

———— • ♦ • ————

A friend that you have to buy won't be worth what you have to pay for him, no matter what that may be.

— *George Prentice*

———— • ♦ • ————

Faithful friends are hard to find:
Every man will be thy friend,
While thou hast wherewith to spend.
— *William Shakespeare*

———— • ♦ • ————

Friendship based solely upon gratitude is like a photograph; with time it fades.

— Carmen Sylva

———— • ♦ • ————

Friendships that have been renewed require more care than those that have never been broken off.

— *Francois de la Rochefoucauld*

[104]

Friendships Remembered

As to the complaints about broken friendship: Friendship is often outgrown; and his former child's clothes will no more fit a man than some of his former friendships.

— Sir Arthur Helps

———— • ◆ • ————

Alas! they had been friends in youth:
But whispering tongues can poison truth,
And constancy lives in realms above;
And life is thorny, and youth is vain,
And to be wroth with one we love
Doth work like madness in the brain.

— Samuel Coleridge

———— • ◆ • ————

It's poor friendship that needs to be constantly bought.

— Proverb

———— • ◆ • ————

What specter can the charnel send
So dreadful as an injured friend?

— Walter Scott

———— • ◆ • ————

He who ceases to be a friend has never been one.

— H. C. Chatfield-Taylor

[105]

You Are My Friend

Cosmus, Duke of Florence, was wont to say of perfidious friends, that "We read that we ought to forgive our enemies; but we do not read that we ought to forgive our friends."

— Francis Bacon

——— • ◆ • ———

The friends who in our sunshine live,
When winter comes are flown;
And he who has but tears to give
Must weep those tears alone.

— Thomas Moore

——— • ◆ • ———

The only danger in friendship is that it will end.

— Thoreau

——— • ◆ • ———

The comfort of having a friend may be taken away, but not that of having had one.

— Seneca

——— • ◆ • ———

No more thy friendship soothes to rest
This weary spirit, tempest tossed:
The cares that weigh upon my breast
Are doubly felt since thou art lost.

— Charlotte Smith

[106]

Friendships Remembered

There is no friend at hand to console me, none who with conversation will beguile the slowly passing time.

— Ovid

———— • ◆ • ————

From decayed fortunes every flatterer shrinks;
Men cease to build where the foundation sinks.
— John Webster

———— • ◆ • ————

Nae man can be happy without a friend, nor be sure of him till he's unhappy.

— Scottish Proverb

———— • ◆ • ————

Virtue, how frail it is!
Friendship, how rare!
— Percy Bysshe Shelley

———— • ◆ • ————

Faint friends when they fall out most cruel foemen be.
— Edmund Spenser

———— • ◆ • ————

Affection once extinguished can lead to nothing but indifference or contempt.

— Honoré de Balzac

You Are My Friend

With a little more patience and a little less temper, a gentler and wiser method might be found in almost every case; and the knot that we cut by some fine heady quarrel-scene in private life, or, in public affairs, by some denunciatory act against what we are pleased to call our neighbor's vices, might yet have been unwoven by the hand of sympathy.

— *Robert Louis Stevenson*

———— • ♦ • ————

And hearts, so lately mingled, seem
Like broken clouds—or like the stream
That smiling left the mountain's brow,
    As though its waters ne'er could sever,
Yet, ere it reach the plain below
Breaks into floods, that part for ever.

— *Thomas Moore*

———— • ♦ • ————

The dissolutions of personal friendship are among the most painful occurrences in human life.

— *Thomas Jefferson*

———— • ♦ • ————

He preserved in the day of poverty and distress that consolation of all this world's afflictions,—a friend.

— *Henry W. Longfellow*

[108]

Friendships Remembered

Friendship's the privilege
Of private men; for wretched greatness knows
No blessing so substantial.
— *Nahum Tate*

———— • ♦ • ————

He that wrongs his friend
Wrongs himself more, and ever bears about
A silent court of justice in his breast.
— *Alfred Lord Tennyson*

———— • ♦ • ————

There is no folly equal to that of throwing away
friendship in a world where friendship is so rare.
— *Edward Bulwer Lytton*

———— • ♦ • ————

My friend! my friend! to address thee delights me,
there is such clearness in the delivery. I am delivered
of my tale, which, being told to strangers, still would
linger in my life as if untold, or doubtful how it ran.
— *Henry David Thoreau*

———— • ♦ • ————

All religion is summed up in the idea of friendship
and friendliness: They make the parable of the Good
Samaritan, the Sermon on the Mount, and the Golden
Rule itself.
— *Brewster Matthews*

You Are My Friend

Where a man cannot fitly play his own part, if he have not a friend he may quit the stage.
— *Francis Bacon*

——— • ♦ • ———

Never let us think that the time can come when we shall lose our friends. Glory, literature, philosophy, have this advantage over friendship: remove one object from them and others fill the void; remove one from friendship, one only, and not the earth, nor the university of worlds, no, nor the intellect that soars above and comprehends them, can replace it.
— *Walter Savage Landor*

——— • ♦ • ———

When care is on me, earth a wilderness,
   The evening starless and unsunned the day,
   When I go clouded like them, sad and grey,
My fears grown mighty and my hope grown less;
When every lilting tune brings new distress,
   Unmirthful sound the children at their play,
   Nor any book can charm my thought away
From the deep sense of mine unworthiness;

Then think I on my friends. Such friends have I,
   Witty and wise, learned, affectionate,
There must be in me something fine and high
   To hold such treasures at the hands of fate;
Their nobleness hints my nobility,
   Their love arrays my soul in robes of state.
— *Wallace Rice*

[110]

Friendships Remembered

To have a friend, to talk with him, is bliss;
But oh, how blest are friendship's silences!
— *Christopher Bannister*

——— • ◆ • ———

Life hath no blessing like a prudent friend.
— *Euripides*

——— • ◆ • ———

I am glad I learned to love the things
That fortune neither takes nor brings;
I am glad my spirit learned to prize
The smiling face of sunny skies;
'T was well I clasped with doting hand
The balmy hedge-flowers of the land:
For still ye live in friendship sure,
My old companions fair and pure.
— *Eliza Cook*

——— • ◆ • ———

'T is something to be willing to commend;
But my best praise is that I am your friend.
— *Southerne*

——— • ◆ • ———

Your friendship is like the spring in the desert,
that never fails; and it is this which makes it impossible
not to love you.
— *Madam de Stael*

[111]

You Are My Friend

Causes best friended have the best event.

— *Heywood*

———— • ♦ • ————

Oh, no doubt, my good friends, but the gods themselves have provided that I shall have much help from you: how had you been my friends else? why have you that charitable title from thousands, did not you chiefly belong to my heart? I have told more of you to myself than you can with modesty speak in your own behalf; and thus far I confirm you. O you gods, think I, what need we have any friends, if we should ne'er have need of 'em? they were the most needless creatures living, should we ne'er have use for 'em, and would most resemble sweet instruments hung up in cases, that keep their sounds to themselves. Why, I have often wished myself poorer, that I might come nearer to you. We are born to do benefits; and what better or properer can we call our own than the riches of our friends?

— *William Shakespeare*

———— • ♦ • ————

Flowers are lovely; Love is flower-like;
Friendship is a sheltering tree;
O! the joys, that came down shower-like,
Of Friendship, Love, and Liberty,
Ere I was old.
— *Samuel Taylor Coleridge*

[112]

Friendships Remembered

And thou shalt prove a shelter to thy friends,
A hoop of gold to bind thy brothers in.
— William Shakespeare

———— • ♦ • ————

Friendship! mysterious cement of the soul!
Sweet'ner of life, and solder of society!
— Robert Blair

———— • ♦ • ————

Friendship is the only point in human affairs, concerning the benefit of which, all men with one voice agree.

— Cicero

———— • ♦ • ————

You do surely bar the door upon your own liberty, if you deny your griefs to your friend.
— William Shakespeare

———— • ♦ • ————

Friendship can smooth the front of rude despair.
— Cambridge

———— • ♦ • ————

A pure friendship inspires, cleanses, expands, and strengthens the soul.

— William Alger

[113]

You Are My Friend

A faithful friend is the medicine of life; for what cannot be effected by means of a true friend? or what utility, what security, does he not afford? What pleasure has friendship? The mere beholding him diffuses an unspeakable joy, and at the bare memory of him the mind is elevated.

— *Saint John Chrysostom*

———— • ♦ • ————

The wise eke saith, woe him that is alone,
For, an he fall, he hath no help to rise.

— *Chaucer*

———— • ♦ • ————

At the need the friend is known.

— *Caxton*

———— • ♦ • ————

As bees mixed nectar draw from fragrant flower,
Do men from friendship wisdom and delight.

— *Edward Young*

———— • ♦ • ————

The greatest benefit which one friend can confer upon another, is to guard, and excite, and elevate his vitures.

— *Samuel Johnson*

[114]

Friendships Remembered

This communicating of a man's self to his friend works two contrary effects, for it redoubleth joys, and cutteth griefs in halves. For there is no man that imparteth his joys to his friend but he enjoyeth the more, and no man that imparteth his griefs to his friend but he grieveth the less.

— *Francis Bacon*

——— • ◆ • ———

Like gushing water brooks,
Freshening and making green and dimmest nooks
Of thy friend's soul thy kindness should flow.
— *James Russell Lowell*

——— • ◆ • ———

You cannot find a man who fully loves any living thing, that, dolt and dullard though he be, is not in some spot lovable himself. He gets something from his friend if he had nothing at all before.

— *Phillips Brooks*

——— • ◆ • ———

Think of the importance of friendship in the education of men. It will make a man honest; it will make him a hero; it will make him a saint. It is the state of the just dealing with the just; the magnanimous with the magnanimous; the sincere with the sincere; man with man.

— *Henry David Thoreau*

You Are My Friend

How sweet, how passing sweet is solitude!
But grant me still a friend in my retreat,
Whom I may whisper—"Solitude is sweet."
— *La Bruyère*

———— • ◆ • ————

When to the sessions of sweet silent thought
  I summon up remembrance of things past,
I sigh the lack of many a thing I sought,
  And with old woes new wail my dear time's waste;
Then can I drown an eye, unused to flow,
  For precious friends hid in death's dateless night,
And weep afresh love's long since cancelled woe,
  And moan the expense of many a vanished sight.
Then can I grieve at grievances foregone,
  And heavily from woe to woe tell o'er
The sad account of fore bemoaned moan,
  Which I now pay as if not paid before:
But if the while I think on thee, dear friend,
All losses are restored, and sorrows end.
— *William Shakespeare*

———— • ◆ • ————

Friendship is more than cattle;
A friend in court aye better is
Than penny is in purse certes.
— *Chaucer*

———— • ◆ • ————

Friendship is the cordial of life, the lentitive of our
sorrows, the multiplier of our joys.
— *Robert Hall*

Friendships Remembered

A true friend is distinguished in the crisis of hazard and necessity, when the gallantry of his aid may show the worth of his soul and loyalty of his heart.

— *Ennius*

———— • ◆ • ————

A principal fruit of friendship is the ease and discharge of the fullness and swellings of the heart, which passions of all kind do cause and induce. We know diseases of stoppings and suffocations are the most dangerous in the body; and it is not much otherwise in the mind. You may take sarza to open the liver, steel to open the spleen, flowers of sulphur for the lungs, castoreum for the brain; but no receipt openeth the heart but a true friend, to whom you may impart griefs, joys, fears, hopes, suspicions, counsels, and whatsoever lieth upon the heart to oppress it, in a kind of civil shift or confession.

— *Francis Bacon*

———— • ◆ • ————

My friends had failed one by one,
Middle-aged, young, and old,
Till the ghosts were warmer to me
Than my friends that had grown cold.
— *Christina Rossetti*

You Are My Friend

Life is to be fortified by many friendships.
To love and to be loved, is the greatest happiness of existence.
— *Sydney Smith*

———— • ♦ • ————

How can life be worth living, if devoid
Of the calm trust reposed by friend in friend?
What sweeter joy than in the kindred soul,
Whose converse differs not from self-communion.
— *Ennius*

12

In Praise Of Friends

I awoke this morning with a devout thanksgiving
for my friends, the old and the new.
       — *Ralph Waldo Emerson*

———— • ◆ • ————

The scampering squirrel, when the Autumn's gift
  Of opening chestnuts and sweet mast descends,
  Bestows them in the keep the poplar lends
Against the wind that sets the snows adrift;
And the lithe branches to the sunlight lift
  Their length unburdened now, each bough unbends
  and raises hands on high, till Heaven sends
Their prayer its answer in the season's shift.
       — *Wallace Rice*

———— • ◆ • ————

And though a coat may a button lack,
And though a face be sooty and black,
And though the words be heavy of flow,
And the new-called thoughts come tardy and slow,
And though rough words in a speech may blend,
A heart's heart, and a friend's a friend.
       — *Will Carleton*

[119]

You Are My Friend

Many kinds of fruit grow upon the tree of life, but none so sweet as friendship.
— Lucy Larcom

———— • ♦ • ————

Friendship is the great chain of human society.
— James Howell

———— • ♦ • ————

You may not know my supreme happiness at having one on earth whom I can call friend.
— Charles Lamb

———— • ♦ • ————

The love of friendship is the most perfect form of love.
— Cardinal Manning

———— • ♦ • ————

Of all felicities the most charming is that of a firm and gentle friendship.
— Seneca

———— • ♦ • ————

Because nature cannot be changed, true friendships are eternal.
— Cicero

[120]

In Praise of Friends

Ardent in its earliest tie,
Faithful in its latest sigh,
Love and Friendship, godlike pair,
Find their throne of glory there.
— *Eliza Cook*

———— • ♦ • ————

Love is deemed the tenderest of our affections, as even the blind and deaf know; but I know, what few believe, that true friendship is more tender still.
— *Count von Platen*

———— • ♦ • ————

God will not love thee less because men love thee more.
— *Martin Tupper*

———— • ♦ • ————

There is indeed no blessing of life that is in any way comparable to the enjoyment of a discreet and virtuous friend.
— *Joseph Addison*

———— • ♦ • ————

There are evergreen men and women in the world, praise be to God!—not many of them, but a few. The sun of our prosperity makes the green of their friendship no brighter, the frost of our adversity kills not the leaves of their affection.
— *Jerome K. Jerome*

[121]

You Are My Friend

Friendship is a crystal lake, sheltered from ruffling winds, wherein he who looks may see his better nature.

— *Christopher Bannister*

——— • ◆ • ———

A happy bit hame this auld world would be,
If men, when they're here, could make shift to agree,
An' ilk said to his neighbor, in cottage an' ha',
"Come gi'e me your hand, we are brethren a'."

— *Robert Nicoll*

——— • ◆ • ———

A friend may well be reckoned the masterpiece of Nature.

— *Ralph Waldo Emerson*

——— • ◆ • ———

Eye lights eye in good friendship, great hearts expand
And grow one in the sense of this world's life.

— *Robert Browning*

——— • ◆ • ———

How many different kinds of friends there are! They should be held close at any cost; for, although some are better than others perhaps, a friend of whatever kind is important; and this one learns as one grows older.

— *John D. Rockefeller*

[122]

In Praise of Friends

What is the odds so long as the fire of souls is kindled at the taper of conwiviality, and the wing of friendship never moults a feather?

— *Charles Dickens*

——— • ◆ • ———

Friendship is the wine of life.

— *Young*

——— • ◆ • ———

Without friendship, society is but meeting.

— *Bacon*

——— • ◆ • ———

Friendship is precious, not only in the shade, but in the sunshine of life; and thanks to a benevolent arrangement of things, the greater part of life is sunshine.

— *Thomas Jefferson*

——— • ◆ • ———

But the best is the clasped hands of comrades when nightfall is near.
Then best is the rest and the friendship, the calm of the soul,
When the stars are in the heaven and the runner lies down at the goal.

— *Richard Hovey*

[123]

You Are My Friend

Oh! let us be happy when friends gather round us.
  However the world may have shadowed our lot;
When the rose-braided links of affection have bound us.
  Let the cold chains of earth be despised and forgot.
And say not that friendship is only ideal;
  That truth and devotion are blessings unknown:
For he who believes every heart is unreal,
  Has something unsound at the core of his own.
Oh! let us be happy when moments of pleasure
  Have brought to our presence the dearest and best;
For the pulse ever beats a most heavenly measure
  When love and good will sweep the strings of the breast.

— *Eliza Cook*

——— • ◆ • ———

Of all the heavenly gifts that mortal men commend,
What trusty treasure in the world can countervail a friend?

— *Nicholas Grimaldi*

——— • ◆ • ———

All money's lost that goes
To an evil wife, or foes'
But on a faithful friend
You gain whate'er you spend.

— *Plautus*

——— • ◆ • ———

A friendship that like love is warm;
A love like friendship, steady.

— *Thomas Moore*

[124]

In Praise of Friends

The sense of sharing makes the blessedness of friendship; strength and invigoration spring from the contact of soul with soul. All beautiful, helpful, inspirational attributes of humanity flourish in the soil of friendship, exerting their beneficence, not only from friend to friend, but over all who may be reached by the expanding grace of goodness and the glad willingness of love. True friendship, therefore, carries with it an enlargement of the faculties and a more extensive life. It shows us the abundance of the world, and makes us feel that it is good.

— *Bertha Gaus*

——— • ◆ • ———

It is like taking the sun out of the world to bereave human life of friendship.

— *Cicero*

——— • ◆ • ———

A friend is more necessary than either fire or water.

— *Taverner's Proverbs*

——— • ◆ • ———

Comradeship is one of the finest facts, and one of the strongest forces in life.

— *Hugh Black*

[125]

You Are My Friend

True love is rare; true friendship, still rarer.
— *Jean de la Fontaine*

———— • ◆ • ————

A faithful friend is a thing most worth.
— *Tottel*

———— • ◆ • ————

No one is so accursed by fate,
No one so utterly desolate,
But some heart, though unknown,
Responds unto his own.
— *Henry W. Longfellow*

———— • ◆ • ————

Friendship, somehow, twines through all lives,
and leaves no mode of being without its presence.
— *Cicero*

———— • ◆ • ————

A friend's bosom
Is the inmost cave of our own mind,
Where we sit from the wide gaze of day
And from the all-communicating air.
— *Percy Bysshe Shelley*

———— • ◆ • ————

Friendship is rarer than love, and more enduring.
— *H.C. Chatfield-Taylor*

[126]

In Praise of Friends

How above all other possessions is the value of a friend in every department of life without any exception whatsoever!

— *John D. Rockefeller*

——— • ♦ • ———

O friendship, equal poised control,
O heart, with kindliest motion warm,
O sacred essence, other form,
O solemn ghost, O crowned soul!

— *Alfred Lord Tennyson*

——— • ♦ • ———

He who is a friend, loves. He who loves is not always a friend. So friendship profits always; but love sometimes is hurtful.

— *Seneca*

——— • ♦ • ———

Some liken their love to the beautiful rose,
    And some to the violet; sweet in the shade;
But the Flower Queen dies when the summer day goes,
    And the blue eye shuts when the spring blossoms fade!
So we'll choose for our emblem a sturdier thing,
    We will go to the mountain and worship its tree;
With a health to the Cedar—the Evergreen King—
    Like that Evergreen so may our friendship be.

— *Eliza Cook*

You Are My Friend

There is nothing that is meritorious but virtue and friendship, and, indeed, friendship itself is but a part of virtue.

— *Alexander Pope*

——— • ♦ • ———

Angels from friendship gather half their joys.

— *Edward Young*

——— • ♦ • ———

Tell me not of sparkling gems,
Set in regal diadems,
You may boast your diamonds rare,
Rubies bright, and pearls so fair;
But there's a peerless gem on earth,
Of richer ray and purer worth;
'T is priceless, but 't is worn by few
It is, it is the heart that's true.

— *Eliza Cook*

——— • ♦ • ———

Honest men esteem and value nothing so much in this world as a real friend. Such a one is as it were another self, to whom we impart our most secret thoughts, who partake of our joy, and comfort us in our affliction; add to this that his company is an everlasting pleasure to us.

— *Pilpay*

[128]

In Praise of Friends

If it is not perfectly understood what virtue there is in friendship and concord, it may be learned from dissension and discord.

— *Cicero*

———— • ◆ • ————

Small service is true service while it lasts.
　　Of humblest friends, bright creature! scorn not one:
The daisy, by the shadow that it casts,
　　Protects the lingering dewdrop from the sun.
— *William Wordsworth*

———— • ◆ • ————

My friend, with you to live alone,
Were how much better than to own
A crown, a sceptre and a throne!
— *Alfred Lord Tennyson*

———— • ◆ • ————

I know you are my friend, and all I dare
Speak to my soul that will I trust with thee.
— *Percy Bysshe Shelley*

———— • ◆ • ————

Let thy soul strive that still the same
Be early friendship's sacred flame.
The affinities have strongest part
In youth, and draw men heart to heart.
—*Dante Gabriel Rossetti*

You Are My Friend

When a beloved hand is laid in ours,
When, jaded with the rush and glare
Of the interminable hours,
Our eyes can in another's eyes read clear,
When our world deafened ear
Is by the tones of a loved voice caressed,
A bolt is shot back somewhere in our breast,
And a lost pulse of feeling stirs again.
The eyes sink inward and the heart lies plain,
And what we mean, we say, and what we would, we know.
A man becomes aware of his life's flow,
And hears its winding murmur and he sees
The meadows where it glides, the sun, the breeze
— *Matthew Arnold*

——— • ◆ • ———

Friendship's like music; two strings tuned alike
Will stir, though only one you strike.
It blooms and blossoms both in sun and shade,
Doth (like a bay in Winter) never fade.
It loveth all and yet suspecteth none,
Is provident, yet seeketh not its own;
'T is rare itself, yet maketh all things common;
And judicious, yet judgeth no man.
— *Francis Quarles*

——— • ◆ • ———

The blood of kindred or affinity
So much not binds us as the friendship pledged
To them that are not of our blood.
— *Algernon Swinburne*

[130]

In Praise of Friends

Best friend,—my well-spring in the wilderness.
— *George Eliot*

———— • ♦ • ————

O Traveler, who hast wandered far
'Neath southern sun and northern star,
Say where the fairest regions are?
Friend, underneath whatever skies,
Love looks in love returning eyes
There are the bowers of Paradise.
— *Clinton Scollard*

———— • ♦ • ————

Who talks of common friendship? There is no such thing in the world. On earth no word is more sublime.

— *Henry Drummond*

———— • ♦ • ————

But sweeter none than voice of faithful friend;
Sweet always, sweetest heard in loudest storm.
Some I remember, and will ne'er forget.
— *Robert Pollock*

———— • ♦ • ————

Nothing in the world is more excellent than friendship.

— *Cicero*

[131]

You Are My Friend

A friend is worth all the hazards we can run.
> — *Edward Young*

——— • ◆ • ———

Friendship is love with understanding.
> — *Proverb*

——— • ◆ • ———

The thread of our life would be dark, Heaven knows!
If it were not with friendship and love intertwined.
> — *Thomas Moore*

——— • ◆ • ———

My treasures are my friends.
> — *Constantius*

——— • ◆ • ———

I count myself in nothing else so happy
As in a soul remembering my good friends,
> — *William Shakespeare*

——— • ◆ • ———

But every road is rough to him that has no friend to
share it.
> — *Elizabeth Shane*

In Praise of Friends

A faithful friend is a true image of the Deity.
— *Napoleon*

——— • ♦ • ———

It's like taking the sun out of the world to bereave human life of friendship.
— *Cicero*

——— • ♦ • ———

Ain't it good to know you've got a friend?
— *James Taylor*

——— • ♦ • ———

It is such a comfort to have a friend near, when lonesome feels do come.
— *Opal Whiteley*

INDEX

Index

Index

Index

Index

Spencer, H., 70
Spenser, E., 30, 107
Stein, G., 73
Stevenson, Robert Louis, 35, 42, 43, 58, 70, 107, 108
Stowe, Harriet B., 16, 60
Streamer, V., 3
Suard, 52
Swift, J., 6, 67, 70, 80
Swinburne, Algernon, 130
Sylva, Carmen, 104

T

Taheb, Ali, 72
Tate, N., 109
Taylor, Jeremy, 15, 29, 30, 61, 95, 133
Tennyson, Alfred, 36, 80, 109, 127, 129
Theophratus, 70
Thomson, J., 12
Thoreau, Henry David, 17, 26, 29, 32, 34, 36, 60, 77, 92, 106, 109, 115
Tottel, 126
Twain, Mark, 27

U

Uhland, L., 103
Upson, A., 43

V

Vanbrugh, J., 103
von Geibel, E., 79
von Platen, C., 121

W

Wallace, H., 14
Wallace, L., 9
Walpole, Hugh, 97
Warner, J.J., 19
Washington, George, 2, 12
Watts-Dunton, H., 36
Webster, J., 93
Weil, Simone, 23
Whiteley, Q., 133
Whiting, L., 52
Wightman, E., 21
Wilcox, Edna W., 48
Wirt, W., 87
Wooster, B., 23
Wordsworth, Wm., 129
Worthington, H., 23
Wycherly, W., 40

Y

Yeats, Wm. Butler, 91
Young, E., 66, 114, 123, 127, 132

WE WELCOME
YOUR COMMENTS

The editors of Halo Books are interested in your comments and suggestions.

Do you know other worthy words of friendship? Let us hear from you.

Write to Halo Books, Box 2529, San Francisco, CA 94126.